Judge John Carro
"The Nuyorican"
A Memoir

John Carro

Judge John Carro - "The Nuyorican" -
A Memoir

Copyright © 2018 by John Carro

ISBN 978-1-7323093-5-7
Printed in the United States of America

Library of Congress Control Number: 2020933514

Y & Y Publishing
New York, NY
yandypublishing@gmail.com

Ordering Information:
Special discounts are available on quantity
purchases by corporations, associations, educators,
and others. For details, contact the publisher at the
above-listed email address.

Table of Contents

Prologue

Many years after my retirement in 1994, I kept being urged to write about my growing up in New York and my experiences as a judge in the New York State courts. I finally decided to write my recollections of some of the events to import to my readers, what it was like being a young Puerto Rican lawyer starting to develop a practice after my induction in 1956, and my early years in Puerto Rico before coming to the United States in 1937.

I am indebted to the following people who helped and urged me to write, and gave me their support: my cousin Madelyn Burgos and her family, for their aid in importing to me their knowledge about Orocovis, my hometown on the island of Puerto Rico. Having left Puerto Rico at the age of ten, her help was immeasurable in acquainting me with the various barrios and morés at the time I was living there.

Neil Wiesner, an attorney, who as a law student was recommended to me by Dean Haywood Burns of CUNY Law School, clerked for me at the Appellate Division and continued to work for me at the Carro law firm. He has become an indispensible friend and colleague for whom I have the utmost respect and regard. I thank him for his aid in the writing and development of this book.

Lizette Cantres and her husband Ramon Rodriguez, former legal aid, attorneys and friends whose marriage ceremony I performed almost thirty years ago. Five years ago, they looked me up and ended up offering to help me with my book. I want to thank Lizette, who helped in the transcription and development of this book. Without that help, this book would not have happened. I am deeply appreciative of her endeavors and for Ramon's counsel.

My family, wife and children, and friends for their unswerving support without which this work would not have been possible.

I want to honor my dearest friend Dr. Frank Bonilla,[1] who was the godfather of my daughter, Christine. He was my hero and best friend for over fifty years. Frank was always there for me and I consider him the most intelligent, trustworthy and caring person that I ever met. Unfortunately, he died before he could write about his own

---

[1] Died in 1986 at the age of 85 in San Diego, California. A memorial was held for him at Hunter College where he taught for twenty years.

experiences. He is my hero, the one who took me out of the ghetto and introduced me to the community at large. Whenever I engage in anything of consequence, politically or otherwise, I always had the steadfast support of Frank whom I trusted without reservation.

Foreword

In November 1937, I left Puerto Rico for New York aboard the Borínquen, one of several steamships that regularly made the voyage between San Juan and New York City.[2] I was ten years old. My father took me to the Port of San Juan where I boarded the ship that would take me to my mother, who had preceded me to New York the previous year. It was only the second time in my life that I had been to San Juan. Before I departed, my father handed me the princely sum of $2.00. I seldom saw him and he did not support my mother nor me, so adding the parting gift to the 52 cents he had contributed earlier brought the total of his financial support so far to $2.52. It was a harrowing five-day voyage. After an hour at sea, while San Juan Harbor was still in sight, I became sea sick. I spent the entire voyage lying on my bunk. I managed to get up once to try to go to the dining room but promptly became violently ill and had to return to my bunk. I couldn't take any food, so I subsisted on soda crackers and water with

---

[2] The steamships included the Coamo, Borinquen, the San Jacinto and, later, the Marine Tiger. In 1942, the Coamo was torpedoed by a German U-boat while returning from transporting troops to Britain and North Africa. It sank and no one aboard survived. Larsson, Bjorn (2012). *Maritime Timetable Images. timetableimages.com/index.htm.*

lemon for the rest of the trip. When I finally arrived in New York City to meet my mother, I was a very frightened little boy.

My mother, Josefina Torres Rivera, was the pioneer in the family. She was in her twenties when she left Puerto Rico and sailed alone to New York to seek work and a better life for us. She had only a third-grade education, spoke no English, and had no vocation. She found work as a sewing machine operator in the garment industry, although she had no experience sewing. It was the height of the Depression on the island.[3] We had no relatives in New York and we knew only one person who lived there: my godmother, María Díaz, but we did not even know her address.

When I first arrived, there were relatively few migrants from Puerto Rico in New York. There had been two modest waves of Puerto Ricans who came, first in the twenties and then in the thirties. They were known collectively as the "Pioneros".[4] As Puerto Ricans began coming to New York in greater numbers, they settled in "El Barrio" (Spanish or East Harlem) in Manhattan: an area that stretched

---

[3] The Stricken Land, Rexford Guy Tugwell
[4] Félix V. Matos-Rodríguez and Pedro Juan Hernández, *Pioneros: Puerto Ricans in New York City 1898-1948*, South Carolina: Arcadia Publishing 2001.

from 100th to 116th and from Lexington Avenue to Fifth Avenue. Many of the newly arrived Puerto Ricans spoke no English and had few marketable skills. Women were absorbed more quickly than men into the workforce because the garment industry in New York was a thriving industry, but unskilled men seemed to have difficulty finding work.

Like many of New York's immigrant enclaves, El Barrio was largely a self-sustaining community. Puerto Ricans had their own movie theaters: the Eagle on 103rd Street and Third Avenue, the Madison (otherwise known as *"el meaíto,"* loosely translated as "the piss pot") which was located on 113th Street and Madison Avenue, the Star on 106th and Lexington Avenue, and a Spanish movie house called "Campo Amor" on 116th and Fifth Avenue. Many Puerto Rican "bodegas", or grocery stores, sprouted up throughout the neighborhoods. Under the tracks of the Metro North commuter train, there was one large supermarket that extended from 111th Street to 115th Street on Park Avenue called "La Marqueta", which was a bustling place where vendors sold fruits, vegetables, fish and live poultry and other staples from their stands.

I spent my early years in el Barrio. I first went to school there and as I grew up, I participated in the street life, the communal activities and the politics. I watched as the Puerto Rican population grew from a handful of immigrants to over one million people in the 1970's.[5] During this time, neighborhoods inhabited by Puerto Ricans expanded down to the Lower East Side and up to the South Bronx, Washington Heights, and out to Williamsburg.

The trajectory of my life has been such that it coincided with the emergence of New York City's Puerto Rican community. As someone who was not only a witness to this history, but who helped shape it, I have often been asked to write about what it was like at this stage of the Puerto Rican migration. Little has been written from the point of view of someone who lived through this era. I have a great many stories to tell and I relate them to give voice to the tales of a million people who share this history. I offer this chronicle of one life as an example to those Puerto Ricans who came after me and to anyone who is interested in a personal account of life as it was for us. In the end, I hope that my recollections and adventures will inform and entertain you.

---

[5] Virgina E. Sánchez Korrol, *From Colonia to Community: The History of Puerto Ricans in New York City*, Berkely: University of California Press 1983, 213.

Chapter One
Backwater Town

To begin with, I was born in a tiny, mountain town in Puerto Rico called Orocovis, a name that comes from the Taíno Indian chief, *Orocovix*[6]. Orocovis is situated in the center of the island, called "el corazón" or "heart", and was once known as "Barros". The town is located between mountains, at the bottom of the foothills. In the twenties and thirties, it was sparsely populated and there were few roads. People still rode on horseback and there was little by way of travel except for a few buses or cars. The only roads that existed were those originally built by the Spaniards. The name "barros" referred to a kind of red clay that endures in the area. At some point, the inhabitants took a dislike to the name and changed it to Orocovis, a reference to the town's Taíno heritage.

Five roads led out of the town; they were the roads that led to Corozal, Baranquitas, Damián, Morovis and Coamo. There were two bridges on

---

[6] The Taíno were aboriginal people who migrated from Venezuela and began to settle in the Caribbean around 400 B.C. Within fifty years of the arrival of the Spanish in 1942, 85 per cent of the population vanished, largely due to disease and privation. Poole, Robert M., *What Became of the Taíno?* Smithsonian Magazine October 2011.

which to exit from the town, a church around which the center of the town was built, and a river that meandered alongside. On those evenings when there were novenas, religious celebrations in the church, the plaza provided recreation for the people who strolled around it. After the novena, the people would promenade around the plaza until about 9:00 or 10:00 PM, and then simply go home. There were no movies, no television, and there were few, if any, radios.

I was born in an area of town called La Pica, which was on the road to Damián, one of the barrios of Orocovis. In addition to "La Pica", there was a neighboring area called "El Cerro", where the poor people lived in shacks surrounding a hill. El Cerro, which has since been demolished, had no running water except for an occasional water pipe. As is often the case in remote areas, the population of Orocovis was homogeneous. There was one black family, as this was a time when most black Puerto Ricans lived on the coasts, near the ocean in the areas of Carolina, Ponce and Guayama. Few people migrated to central Puerto Rico, where they largely grew coffee, plátanos, guinéos, tobacco and corn, and there was little employment.

As a child, I assumed that the entire world was Puerto Rican, since the Mayor of the town was

Puerto Rican, the doctor was Puerto Rican and everyone else seemed to be Puerto Rican, except for the parish priest. His name was Martin Barry and let it be known that he was from Ireland. We were mostly Catholic with a few Protestants.

Orocovis had two elementary schools called Escuela Pedro Arroyo and Escuela Felipe Carro that covered grades one to six. If you wanted to go further, to a junior high school or high school, you had to go to an adjoining towns as Barranquitas or Corozal, which were over a half hour away. As a result, most children went no further than the sixth grade. My own parents went only as far as the third grade. There was also one pharmacy, a post office but no hospital. There was no electricity, so we lived by gaslights, or *quinques*, candles. Most people came to town on horseback. Although the town had 17 barrios,[7] or suburbs, the lack of transportation made it very hard to travel between them. When it rained, it was almost impossible to go from one area to another by horseback because it was so hilly and muddy. Orocovis was the proverbial backwater town.

---

[7] Barrios: 1) Botijas, 2) Damian Arriba, 3) Damian Abajo, 4) El Gato, 5) Cacao, 6) Matrulla, 7) Barros, 8) Mata de Caña, 9) Boate, 10) Bervejales, 11) Ala de la Piedra, 12) Sabana, Grande, 13) Bauta Arriba, 14) Bauta Abajo, 15) Collores, and 16) El Salto de Cabras

There were no factories in Orocovis and people relied on what they grew for nourishment. Some lived on whatever they could earn as sharecroppers. During the Great Depression, the United States government provided some measure of economic assistance through programs like those of the Puerto Rican Emergency Relief Administration (La PRERA), a New Deal program designed to stimulate growth in agriculture and to build infrastructure. In Orocovis, people raised animals, chickens, goats and pigs. Beef was scarce but there were a variety of tropical vegetables called, collectively, *viandas.* They included *plátanos, yautías, malangas, apios, guinéos verdes* (green bananas), which, along with rice and beans as a staple, constituted what people ate daily. There were no refrigerators, so the little meat that was available was dried. One form of dried beef was *ropa viéja,* "old clothes" or *tasajo.* People also ate dried codfish, *bacalao,* which was customarily served on "meatless" Fridays to comply with Catholic doctrine.

The river was an important source of food and perhaps also the greatest source of recreation. The river's fresh water came from the rain and the mountains. When it rained a great deal, the two bridges leading to the town frequently flooded, sometimes washing away cars, houses, animals and anything you owned. The river provided fresh water shrimp called *guábaras, bruquenas* —a small type of shellfish—and *camarones*—regular small and large shrimp. People could catch fish by turning over rocks or just holding a burlap sack in the water of the river as it flowed. You were able to catch enough fish to cook right there at the river and make lunch along with the viandas. One hazard of the river was the *abispas*, which are wasps. Whatever part of your body they stung: your hands, your face, your legs, your torso, it would swell. The common antidote for an abispa bite was urine mixed with mud or dirt, which somehow reduced the swelling.

Despite the lack of transportation, some people did manage to work in other places, larger towns where there were factories. But, as a rule, people worked as sharecroppers on land owned by the Carro's—my father's family, and the other property-owning families. In Orocovis, people had their own houses; small houses were rarely more than one story and unlike Puerto Rico today, they were not built from cement. In those days, houses were made out of wood and the roofs were made of zinc. There were no glass windows. The porch area was called the *batey*, nothing more than the smoothed earth in front of the house that you polished with a broom. The furniture generally consisted of *sillones* (armchairs), *sillas* (chairs) and the occasional hammock and simple bed. The traditional house had maybe one or two bedrooms and was very small compared to modern houses. Because we lived in the tropics, we dug shelters into the ground called *barrancas* to protect us from the storms. When you heard a storm was coming, you left the house and went to the *barrancas* (shelters). There were two big storms during my childhood: the San Felipe storm which came in 1928, a year after I was born, and the San Ciprian storm, which hit the isalnd in 1932. The storms caused the rivers to overflow and in one case, washed away the church in Ororcovis. The storms brought great calamity, as the water overran the river that led into Orocovis, sweeping up the livestock, houses, chairs, and farm animals. The roads became impassable and it would be several days before you could go in and out of the area.

By any standards, life in Orocovis was one of extreme poverty. Yet somehow, we survived. As children, we rode horses, played cops and robbers, marbles and other childhood games that were typical of the day: "hot peas and butter" and "johnnie-on-the-pony". At night, we played Spanish cards or dominoes. There were no organized sports and no movie houses in Orocovis. Occasionally, a traveling circus or a fair came to town and set up tents, but this would last only a few days.

I started school when I was five. My mother first tried to enroll me at the age of four, but I was too young. They sent me home when I began to cry. I returned to school the following year. When I completed the third grade, I was skipped to the fifth grade. I could only go for another year at my elementary school, which only went to the sixth grade, and there was no school to attend after that. This was when my mother decided to leave Puerto Rico in 1936, to go to New York.

I grew up in a way that was fairly typical for a small town. It was like the young life of Tom Sawyer or Huckleberry Finn, because the river circumscribed my existence. Although Puerto Rico is an island, 35 miles wide by 100 miles long, I never went to a beach because beaches were several miles away from Orocovis. On the rare occasion that I was able to ride in a car on the hazardous roads, I became carsick, so trips to the beach were traumatizing. Initially, I did not know how to swim, which was a problem. I learned to swim in the river the hard way: by being thrown in by my uncle, Luis, who was one of those "sink or swim" guys. One day when I was with Uncle Luis, I was bathing near my grandmother's home in El Charco de las Mujeres, the place where women bathed. My uncle was busy doing somersaults in the water and, attempting to imitate him, I dunked myself in the water. I could not swim—much less do somersaults. Instead, I began to swallow water and to float down the river, drowning. A farmer who was tending to his livestock saw my body floating down the river, walked over and fished me out of the water. My grandmother, Abuela Concha, was summoned. When she heard what had happened, she came down to the river's edge with a machete, cut down some brush and proceeded to whip the water out of me. I survived.

Swimming became the greatest enjoyment of my life. In Puerto Rico you can swim all year round. On a typical day, I would swim in the river at eight o'clock in the morning, before I started school, at lunchtime and after school, I would swim at "El Sabino", the swimming hole behind my Uncle Fernando's store in the town. I spent one summer on a raft made of balsa wood, called *grayumo*, floating down the river and eating *pomarosas*, an apple-like fruit, which is very tasty and hollow inside. It was an idyllic existence and the experience has remained with me.

As an adult, when I returned to Puerto Rico twenty years after I left, I received the greatest shock of my life. I went to Orocovis only to find that the river had all but died. It had dried up. El Sabino and the swimming hole by the school were gone. The river that overflowed in my childhood now barely existed.

To earn money as a boy, I started raising chickens beginning with one chicken and acquiring about fifteen of them. I learned how to feel the chickens to see when they were ready to lay eggs and I would wait around. Each egg I got I would sell for a penny. I loved to eat *fresas*—wild strawberries, although on occasion, I was stung by wasps while picking them. My face and hands would swell up, necessitating the application of the antidote: soaking the swollen part in urine mixed with mud.

When I was seven or eight, I had one of those memorable childhood episodes drinking alcohol. It was Election Day and I went to my Tío Fernando's store in town. He left me minding the store while he went out to vote. While he was gone, I decided to experiment and I smoked a cigarette, tasted rum, rye whiskey, beer, and *mavi,* a drink made from fermented tree bark. I was loaded by the time my uncle returned. I attempted to make it home, with my friend, Tinín Aviles, who lived next to me in La Pica. As we were winding our way there, I passed out in a gully by the road to Corozal. When I woke up, I was in a bed with people praying over me and washing my feet in urine, which seemed to be the all-purpose cure. I thought I was in Heaven since everything looked kind of cloudy to me. I managed to recover, never to indulge again. I have neither smoked a cigarette nor drank a beer since that day and I never drink hard liquor. My life since has been *"pura y sana,"* pure and healthy, as we say in Spanish. I did fall off the wagon once in the Navy when we bought a bottle of Southern Comfort and I unfortunately imbibed to the point where I became as sick as a dog. But since then I have not had alcohol, except that in later years I had an occasional martini with my compadre and dear friend, Frank Bonilla.

Chapter Two
From Whence I Came

Although my mother is the most important person in my life, I know little about her life. I am deeply indebted to my mother. I credit her for all I have achieved in life. In Orocovis, I was surrounded by my mother's family. They provided a support system that made it possible for my mother to leave Puerto Rico and establish a life in New York for me. My mother's mother was Angela Rivera, whom we called Mamá. Mamá had several children among who were my mother, Josefina, the oldest, born between 1908 and 1910. My mother lived until February 9, 1998, one day shy of her ninetieth birthday. Other siblings were Amparo, next to the oldest sister; Rosenda ("Senda"), who was developmentally disabled, although then there was no possibility of a diagnosis or treatment. She was cognitively impaired and was cared for all her short life by the rest of the family. She died in her twenties or thirties. There was another sister, Carmen, and a brother, Angel Luis. My mother also had half brothers, among them Guillermo ("Guillo") and Maximo or Minín, who were the children of Maximino Torres, Don Mino. There was also a half brother Alberto ("Berto"), who had a different father. My grandmother also raised another child as her daughter, Neida, who was placed in her care. Children who could not be cared for in their homes were often taken by others in the community. Mamá had two brothers, Fernándo Burgos (Tío Fernándo), and Charles Rivera (Tío Charles) who were married to sisters, Titi and Andréa.

My great grandmother was Abuela Concha, short for Concepción Miranda. At one point in my life, my mother, my grandmother and my great grandmother were all alive. Abuela Concha had her own house on the road to Corozal. My uncle, Tío Fernando, had married a woman named María and had four children, Rosaura, Lydia, Fernandito, and Neftali, aka Tali. Tío Charles had two children. There was one other brother who moved to Chicago and I never got to know very well. His wife was Tía Rafa and they had several children, among them Pablo or Paco and Surín. I am the only child of mother and my father Juan. My mother's father was Jesús Torres, who was born in Coamo, but I never met him or any of his family.

My father's family were wealthy aristocrats. They were big landowners who were socially prominent. Despite the Carro wealth, my father, who was the illegitimate son of Francisco, one of the Carro brothers, barely acknowledged my existence and never provided any support to my mother and me. It was, in part, my father's neglect that drove my mother to create a life for me that would allow me to succeed. She convinced me that I was the equal of any man, particularly of my father and his family and there was nothing that I could not accomplish. The Carros emigrated from Spain in the late of 1800's, travelling to Argentina, Puerto Rico and Cuba. In Puerto Rico, they settled in the central part of the island in the area around Orocovis and Corozal, purchased land and became prominent landowners. The Carro immediate family consisted of five brothers and a sister, Felipe, the oldest, Tomás, Antonio (Toño), José (Seíto) and Francisco, the youngest of father's brothers. The sister, Providencia, had five daughters, all of whom became doctors and a son, who became a lawyer and a horse breeder.

My father was the illegitimate son of my great grandfather, Don Francisco Carro and I never knew who my father's mother was. The Carros prospered although they had little formal education, except for Felipe, who was a college graduate, and they acquired thousands of acres around Orocovis and Corozal. Felipe, in addition to owning land, opened a canning factory, 'Carro Products', and an elementary school in Orocovis, named, 'Escuela Felipe Carro'. He was a Republican who was elected to the Puerto Rican House of Representatives. Toño was a builder and employed a crew of engineers and workers that built many of the roads in the central part of the island. Tomás was a playboy who gambled, drank and was known for his parties in an area called Mata de Caña, in Corozal. He bred horses and for a time owned a stable of horses, among them prize winning Puerto Rican champions, El Tite and Camarero. Tomás never married but was reputed to have had a child with María Diaz, my godmother. Seíto married late in his seventies and lived in the outskirts of Orocovis, where he raised several children. Word was that, before marrying, he had sired approximately twenty-five children with women from the farm and provided them with houses where they lived off the family land and store.

The Carros established a rancho, akin to a warehouse, where they stacked the tobacco they grew and raised livestock, chickens and pigs. The Carro Family rented land to sharecroppers, who also worked as ranch hands. They also sold Carro Products, processed by Felipe in the canning business and had as many as 26 canned products. He became famous for his *gandules* (pigeon peas) and beans. The business did very well, although it distributed goods only in Puerto Rico. Eventually, the Carro children did not want to be farmers nor work in the family any longer. One of Felipe's sons, Felipe, became a dentist and the others went into medicine and different fields. Only one son, Ramón Luís, remained on the land, grew rich and married a wealthy woman, Elba, a widow, who was left a fortune in jewelry and over 20,000 acres in Coamo. Later, the Carro Products division was bought by Goya Foods, now the largest Spanish and Latin food seller in the US and Puerto Rico.

Other branches of the Carro family from Spain, whom I never met, went to live in Argentina and Cuba. When I later travelled to Cuba, I looked in the phone book and found that there were over twenty Carro surnames, but was never able to contact anyone. Although I had been to Argentina, I understand that branches of the family still live there. The Carros are the only family in Puerto

Rico with that surname, spelled with two r's. Every few years they have a family reunion attended by over 300 Carros- all of whom are the offspring of those five brothers. I was one of the few who came to New York. I have kept in touch with their children and grandchildren and it is always a great experience to go to a Carro get together and meet other members and branches of the family. To date, they have had two Carro family reunions in the last few years.

Chapter Three
El Barrio

When I arrived in New York, I spoke very little English. I had seldom been outside my town of Orocovis, except when my mother and I lived for a short time in Comerío. I had only been to San Juan once, and had become so carsick from the smell of "*mangles*", the seaside areas, where they raised crabs, that I never made it the beach, which was our destination. The first time that I ever visited a beach was when I went to Coney Island.

You cannot imagine what it was like for me to come to New York. I was a child who had never seen buildings taller than two stories and in my homogenous little town. In my mind, everyone was Puerto Rican. I did not know what it was to be Jewish, Italian, German or Irish and had little experience even with black Puerto Ricans. I came to live in a furnished room with my mother on West 112th Street between Fifth and Lenox Avenue, an African-American neighborhood on the border of the El Barrio. My mother rented a room in an apartment for several dollars a week. It provided shelter but we did not have cooking privileges and could only make coffee to drink with our bread. We bought lunch and dinner in *fiambreras*, porcelain lunch boxes made out of three of four stacked casseroles; one containing rice, one bean, another one meat and the other containing salad. The food was quite good and my mother and I were able to subsist mainly on that.

My mother was making less than ten dollars a week working as a seamstress when she came here. Although life was harsh, el Barrio, for me, was a haven where you didn't have to speak English. Commerce was conducted in Spanish and everyone spoke Spanish. But because I had to learn to speak English, I was registered at a school, P.S. 170; in a special class to learn English. After three months I was transferred to a regular class at P.S. 72 elementary school. The school was on 111th Street between Fifth and Lenox Avenue in Manhattan. My first class was a "C" class where I was taught English. Once I learned English, I went to a regular fifth grade class. There were about twenty students in my class, African American children and a few Latinos. At school, I was hit upon by bullies every day after 3:00. Classmates and other students picked fights with me and I would have to fight everyday while someone held my books. On the day that the fifth grade ended, my homeroom teacher, Miss Fishman, was kind enough to send me home early when she heard a classmate threatened to "wait for me outside." In class he had hit me with

a piece of carpet from a zip gun and I fired one
back.

PATRICK HENRY
JUNIOR H.S.
June 1941

Once I made it home safely there would be
bread and coffee that my mother prepared for me to
tie me over until she returned from work, generally
after 5 pm. Apartments and furnished rooms were
plentiful in those days. My mother managed to find
another furnished room in a neighborhood that was
in another school district, which was fortunate for
me because I would not have to attend Junior High
School Cooper, a school with a serious gang
problem. Instead we moved to 1604 Madison
Avenue, at 107th Street and I registered in a school
that was safer and more diverse. P.S. 72, between
105th and 106th Streets and Lexington Avenue, was
a predominantly white school but the students were
a mixture of Italians, Irish and people of all

nationalities, including several Puerto Ricans and a few African Americans. I did so well that I graduated with the highest average in the school for that year, for which I should have received an award. Instead it was given to another boy, Peter Rugneta, who had been there five years. I was a somewhat disappointed but I felt it was a valid reason since I had been there only one year.

Elementary School - 6th Grade

I went on to Junior High School, P.S. 171, on 104th between Madison and Fifth Avenues, which had Rapid Advancement classes. Being placed in the "Rapids" meant that instead of spending a year in each grade, I went to seventh, eighth and ninth grade for only six months each, finishing junior high school in a year and a half. P.S. 171 was a little tougher than going to P.S.72, because there was greater racial conflict. I immediately became the victim of extortion. On the first day I was pushed by a black student when I went to get a free lunch; something I was entitled because I was a poor kid. The boy, Zack Bailey, demanded that I pay him two cents daily to eat free lunch. One day I refused to pay. He pushed me, I pushed him back and he muttered to me that he would see me outside after school. By this time, I had acquired a few Puerto Rican friends. I told them what had happened and they accompanied me outside. When Zach Bailey saw me come out with my boys, he asked me why I hadn't told him I was one of the boys. After that, I didn't have to pay and we became friends. I also developed friendships with two other African American boys, Sidney Jackson and Warren Hardy.

In the meantime, my mother continued to move from one furnished room or apartment to another. In those days the landlord, would give you a month's free rent and other incentives like providing shades or refinishing the floors. Our first apartment was in a great, multi-racial area, on 107th Street, between Madison and Fifth Avenues, where we lived among Irish, Italians, Russian Jews and all kinds of people. I made a number of friends at school, among them Ralph Vicent, Walter Sheppard and Warren Harty. They were bright kids and we did homework together. Unfortunately, my mother who liked to see new apartments, soon found one apartment after the other, so that in the first five years or so that I was in New York, we moved eight or ten times. This was good because we were offered a better deal each time, but for me it was hard to be constantly on the move and have to make new friends.

To help with expenses, I shined shoes at 108th Street and Madison Avenue for ten cents a shine I used what little money I made to go to the Municipal Theater ("El Meáito") where I would buy a pineapple cheese pie for twelve cents, grapes or other fruit and spend three hours at the movies on Saturday afternoons. Movies cost a nickel or a dime and sometimes I would even have a free pass from my local Chinese laundry where they would put up movie posters. During those afternoons I would see two movies, a serial, either Flash Gordon or the Lone Ranger, and some cartoons. My mother gave me a three dollar a week allowance and with the money I earned from my shining shoes and other odd jobs, I bought my own clothes. I began going to parties and I learned to dance. I even bought a Zoot Suit from a store located at 111th Street and Lexington Avenue called Gray Rudder.

Each time I moved to a new place, I would have to start making new friends, but not before being tested as the new kid on the block. Being tested meant that I had to contend with the social group or gang that reigned in that block. These were not the violent gangs that I would encounter years later when I was a youth worker. To become a member, you had to show that you were the kind of person that would not take abuse, but would stand up and fight if you had to. I managed to maintain enough of a bravado so that I had no problem meeting people and making new friends. Once in the gang, we would mostly hang out at the candy stores and hallways and act tough. We had girlfriends and we went dancing but there was no sex in those days. The best we could hope at that time was necking and petting. There was no real drug problem in the forties and no guns. Violence was limited to street fights, brawls, what we called "fair ones." We wore distinctive logos on our jackets or sweaters representing our gang. In the streets, we roller-skated, boxed and played all the usual childhood games, especially stick ball.

Stickball was the main sport of El Barrio. All you needed to play was a broom handle for a bat and a Spalding ball, which had a high bounce. Most blocks had a stickball team. The games were played on the street, using the sewer covers for bases. Teams sprouted up all through the neighborhoods, including the "Home Reliefs," a top team, that played out of 114th Street between Park and Lexington Avenues. There was great competition and the games often drew crowds. The fans bet hundreds of dollars on their favorite teams. Stickball was later introduced to the Bronx, when Puerto Ricans started arriving there and where it is still played today.

The gangs wore signature jackets or sweaters. When I was a Cavalier, whose territory was on 110th Street and Lexington Avenue, I wore a white and silver satin jacket with a top hat insignia. On 112th Street, I belonged to the Zeniths whose jackets were blue and gold. Later, when we moved to 146th Street and Broadway in Washington Heights, I was in the Red Skulls, whose sweaters were black with red borders. Then there were also the Puerto Rican Counts on 136th Street and Broadway, who also wore red and black sweaters.

Our social lives were organized around our gangs. Boxing was popular. It required little experience and there were good fighters throughout El Barrio. While in the Zeniths, I joined the P.A.L. where I learned to box under the aegis of Frank Rodríguez, the coach. Those of us who boxed were highly respected in our neighborhoods and boxing discouraged others from messing with us. We trained at the P.A.L. on 126th and Lexington Avenue and would go routinely to Jamaica, Queens and Long Island to box. I fought at 118 pounds. In Jamaica, we were paid $5.00 per round for each fight, which lasted three rounds. At the gym I met a boxer named Sandy Saddler, who was in the stable of another trainer, Nick Bruno. One day I had the misfortune to spar with Sandy, a left-handed African American fighter who later became featherweight champion of the world, besting Willie Pep whom he fought in Madison Square Garden, 3 times. He was the hardest hitter I ever encountered. When I was sparring with him once, Sandy gave me such a shot that 'I saw the Milky Way'. Despite that, we became good friends, a friendship that lasted through the years.

The peer pressure of gang membership would also lead to making bad decisions. As I approached the end of junior high school, I decided to go to Bronx High School of Science because I wanted to be in a pre-med program and become a doctor. I took the test and passed but then made a choice I would come to regret. I was in the Zeniths then and my friends wanted me to go with them to Benjamin Franklin High School, a new school that was opening on 116th Street and Pleasant Avenue. They persuaded me to go to Benjamin Franklin instead of Bronx Science. Franklin was in the Italian section of East Harlem and on the first day we realized we needed to get past the entire Italian neighborhood to get to school. If we travelled alone, along 114th Street between Lexington and Madison Avenues, we were sure to be attacked, so we went together. There were about thirteen of us in the satin blue and yellow jackets of the Zeniths, and no one bothered us. After the first day my fellow Zeniths began to play hooky and I wound up having gone to school by myself. I learned early the lesson that I should not be swayed by friends. I still believe that if I had gone to Bronx Science, I might have become a doctor.

As I would do often in my life, I made the best of my situation. Going to Benjamin Franklin High turned out not to be so bad after all and I did well there. I formed friendships that proved to be important later in my life; among them a friendship with the principal, Dr. Leonard Covello, a leading Italian scholar, who would be one of my references when I applied for a John Jay Whitney Opportunity Fellowship. I also met the future U.S. senator, Daniel Patrick Moynihan, who was in Dr. Rita Morgan's English class with me. As the Senator from New York, he would come to play a significant role in my life by sponsoring my application to the federal bench for the Southern District of New York.

In high school I decided to take Spanish, because mine had become very poor after years of education policy designed to make students forget their culture and language and join the "melting pot." While the policy succeeded in making us forget Spanish, it was not very successful in teaching us English. At P.S. 171, I studied French for two years under Miss Rouelle. At Franklin High School, I enrolled in the Spanish I class taught by Mrs. Kanheimer. When I walked, the teacher greeted me by saying, in heavy English at "tu eres" (you are) "Hispano-Americano". I looked at her and said, "You're going to teach me Spanish?" I walked out and proceeded to go upstairs to see the head of the Spanish Department, Dr. Pergola. I told him, "That woman can't teach me, she doesn't even speak Spanish well," to which he responded, "What are you, a wise guy?" I explained that I did speak Spanish, but wanted to improve it. He asked a couple of questions and, in fact, gave me a comprehensive exam. I gathered I did well because after the exam he gave me credit for two years of Spanish and I started in third year Spanish, where I had Dr. Emilio Guerra, who turned out to be a terrific teacher. I ended up receiving the language award for Spanish upon my graduation.

I participated in some school activities at Franklin only during the school hours. Although I liked basketball and could have played in the Junior Varsity, I had to work after school to help my mother and could not stay after school. Benjamin Franklin had Bill Spiegel as coach and a championship basketball team. The team was the champion of New York City. The captain of the team was Joe Galiber and Fred Pericas were the team's stars. Joe later became the Captain of the team at City College, the team that at one point won the NCAA and the NIT titles; the only time that ever happened. During the time Joe Galiber was captain, five of the six people, on the team, although not Joe Galiber nor Sherman White of LIU (Long Island

University), were indicted for a so-called corruption scheme. This led to the demise of City College's great coach, Nat Holman and Clair Bee of LIU.

As a member the General Organization (the G.O.) I was asked to run for the school leadership organization, which required a regular campaign for election to the offices of president, vice president and secretary. My slate of candidates took into account the diversity of the school, mainly Italians, some Latinos and blacks, and ran a ticket that included an Italian student, Rudy Cristiano, as candidate for President, a black student, Eugene Boyd, for Vice President and me, running for G.O. Secretary. As part of the campaign, the slate had to present our platform to an assembly of the student body. In my case, this was my first experience ever in public speaking. I sat in the auditorium and made a list of what I wanted to say. Unfortunately, I was the last speaker and by the time my turn came, everything that I had to say had been said. To make matters worse, I was extremely nervous and still spoke with a slight accent. When I got up to speak, I dropped the paper I made notes on, and as it flew away I said, "There goes my speech," which got a laugh. As I proceeded to ad-lib, I learned that I was good at public speaking. We went on to win the election and became the officers of the G.O.

At Franklin, I also experienced an infatuation with a student teacher of Spanish, Stella Rogdakis. Miss Rogdakis befriended me and entered me in an all-city Spanish competition for students from different high schools. I didn't win, but I did manage to spend some time with her. She was a beautiful woman and I became infatuated with her. She also worked with the school band and just to be near her I managed to join the band. I played the *"clave"*, the two sticks that mark the time in Latin music. I also got her to agree that if I won the election for Secretary of the G.O., she would give me a kiss. When we won, the first thing I did was to go to her to get my kiss and she made good on her promise. That crush was one of the highlights of my high school life.

Young people in those days were not as promiscuous as they are now. Although you went on dates, there was very little sex involved. I did not have any sex until I went into the service. Dancing was an outlet for us, it allowed for safe contact between the sexes. I learned to dance at house parties and at the Plaza, a club on 110th Street and Fifth Avenue. Later, I discovered the Royal Manor, on 156th Street and Broadway, where we could dance on Sundays from 6:00 to 10:00 pm. It was at the Royal Manor that I met my first real girlfriend, Terry Parco, who hailed from the Bronx.

I would meet her at the dance and then escort her home by taking the trolley at 155th Street and Amsterdam Avenue that went to the Bronx. I would drop her off at Southern Boulevard. She never allowed me to take her home because her mother was an old fashioned Italian who did not allow her to mix with Puerto Rican boys. She had to be home by 11 p.m. and was afraid of her mother, so my courting her consisted of writing to her, as there were no private phones, meeting her at the dances, dancing with her and escorting her home on the trolley and leaving when the trolley ride ended. I never met her mother or her father, nor she did she meet mine. Neither of us had fathers at home. Terry hand an older sister, Eleanor and a brother, Alfred Parco.

When I met Terry, I was a freshman at Fordham University. She told me she went to a school called John Dwyer and I assumed it was a high school. It turned out that she was much younger than I thought; she was only fourteen and just in junior high school. We had no phones, so I only saw her at the Sunday dances or we would communicate by letter. Once or twice, we went to the movies. Although Terry and I would one day marry, in the beginning our relationship was little more than a case of puppy love. I continued going with Terry until I went into the Navy. As I promised, I kept in touch with her and wrote many letters home, in care of her friend, Yolie, who lived in her building at 957 Aldus Avenue in the Bronx. Her mother did not know we were corresponding by mail.

Chapter Four
Expanding Horizons

In 1941, I graduated from high school in the seventh term, after two and a half years. I was fifteen and living in El Barrio. As my high school graduation approached, I was contemplating going to college. I was then attending the Casita María, a neighborhood settlement house on 110th Street between Madison and Park Avenues. The Casita María was sponsored by the Catholic Church and provided services to Puerto Rican youths who lived in poverty. It was run by Miss Weinig and Miss Elizabeth Ridder, who was sister of Ed Sullivan, a famous variety TV show host.

Casita arranged for the poor young people to go to a summer camp for two weeks under the auspices of the Catholic Youth Organization ("CYO). I was among those selected to go to camp that was located in Spring Valley, New York. Although I was fifteen and was graduating from high school, I was put in with a group of ten to thirteen year olds. One day I borrowed a nickel from one of the younger kids. When he asked me to pay it back, I used a slang term, "bomba" to tell him that I was not going to pay. The Catholic lay brother, in charge of our group, heard me say the word "bomba" and mistakenly thought that I was calling him a bastard. When he slapped me, my street instincts took over. He was a big man so I grabbed a bat and menaced him. He kicked me out of the cabin for the night and I found myself spending the night alone in the dark woods. It was after ten o'clock but as time passed, and I was becoming unaccustomed to being in the woods alone. I sought shelter so that I could sleep and settled upon a makeshift altar set up for the priests to conduct early mass. The altar had a quilt spread on the floor and I lay down and fell asleep.

At about five a.m., the priests came along to prepare for an early mass and they found me asleep on the mat. One of them, whom I later learned was named Orville Griese, woke me up and started a conversation. He told me he was from Wisconsin. I told him my story; that at fifteen I was graduating from high school and planned to attend college; that I needed to earn money but was too young to qualify for working papers. He asked me which college I was applying to and I said City College, because tuition was free. Father Griese told me it was the wrong place to go because City College was full of communists, and if I went there I would jeopardize or even lose my faith. I said "what faith?" and assured him that I was not afraid of losing my faith because I had none to lose.

Father Griese did not give up on me. He kept in touch with me and urged me to go to schools like Catholic University and Georgetown, places I would never consider attending because I would not leave home and miss my mother and my rice and beans. Finally, he contacted me to tell me that I should consider going to Fordham University, a Jesuit school in New York. I knew nothing about Fordham and had a vague idea that it was somewhere in New England. I learned it was in the Bronx and from where I was living in Manhattan it was a simple matter of taking the subway, to Fordham Road. I made my way to Fordham University, which was next to the Bronx Botanical Gardens and the Bronx Zoo. It was a beautiful place, with extensive grounds and wonderful buildings. More importantly, I could commute to Fordham by public transportation. Knowing that I could continue to live with my mother while I attended, I wrote back to Father Griese and said that I would be interested in going to Fordham.

I visited the campus at Fordham, walked around the grounds and met with Father Gannon, who was then President of the school. When I applied to the school, Father Griese contacted Father Gannon, who informed me soon thereafter that Fordham would be admitting me as a freshman in the class of 1947. It was during World War II and many of the students had been drafted. Fordham was then on a trimester schedule of classes, a system developed so that each year had three terms lasting three months each and you could graduate earlier. When I began to attend Fordham, it was a new and strange experience that felt far away from the streets of El Barrio.

I went to school by a city bus that left me on Fordham Road, in front of the school. Although tuition was low, we had to borrow money from my Uncle Luis, who owned a grocery store. At Fordham there was only one other Puerto Rican student, whom I remember because his name was Cruz de Jesús, or Cross of Jesus, something that was hard to forget. There were also two other Latinos, the Karam brothers who were rumored to be rich kids from Venezuela. Everyone else at this conservative Catholic university was Irish or Italian. I enrolled as a pre-med student, but since it was a Jesuit school, I had to take Religion in addition to my science courses and other classes, which ran from 9:00 am to 5:00 pm daily.

It took a while to adjust to the new environment. For one thing, in El Barrio we dressed differently from the boys in college. We wore pegged pants that were narrow at the ankles and then ballooned up. The college students wore corduroy jackets with patches at the elbow, brown and white saddle shoes or penny loafers. It was inevitable that I would be confronted because I was different and dressed differently; after all it was like moving again to yet another "block." On one occasion, I was walking to a Fordham building, Dealy Hall, with books under my arms. I was stopped by four students who asked me where I was going and "where was I from". I told them I was going to Dealy Hall and that I was from Harlem. I asked them the same questions. As I spoke, I pointed my right index finger at them and one of the boys objected. I advised him not to worry about what my right hand was doing because I was left-handed and that was the hand he had to worry about. I was well-schooled in the handling such confrontations, so I dropped my books, took my boxing stance and asked which of them was going to do something about it. The students quickly backed down and apologized and things worked out without any punches being thrown.

On another day I joined a friend of mine, Mike Fumarola, who was in line at the school cafeteria. As I sneaked up in the line I heard someone say, "Where are you going spic?" When I responded by asking, "What did you call me?" He said, "Spic, isn't that what your friend calls you?" I said that what my friend called me was one thing, but that he did not have my permission to call me a spic and that I did not appreciate him doing it. His answer was, "I know about you spics, my father's a cop from Harlem and you spics all carry knives." I turned my pockets inside out to show that I did not carry a knife and asked him if he wanted to make something out of it. He challenged me to fight and I accepted. He was much bigger than I was so it was fortunate when one of my Irish friends, spoke up and said, "Listen John, let me take him," which he did.

There were only a few other incidents at Fordham and I did manage to adapt socially after a period of time. Academically, I had a tough time during my first year at Fordham. My education at Benjamin Franklin High School left me unprepared for college. I had not taken many Regents courses nor had I taken physics, chemistry or math higher than algebra. Many of the students at Fordham came from the more elite Catholic schools, such as Regis, or Xavier where they had taken the courses that you need for college. I was struggling; I had to drop French and take Spanish. My grades for the first trimester averaged under eighty per cent. Fortunately, I became friendly with a young fellow named Jean Baptiste who was French, had come from Cuba and spoke fluent Spanish. He helped me with physics, French, math and the other classes I was taking. By junior and senior years, my grade average had risen to 90%.

At Fordham I developed an interest and a love for English and literature thanks to Professor Liegey. He introduced me to Beowulf, Sir Gawain and the Green Knight, The Decameron and the poets Keats, Byron, Shelley, Donne and Shakespeare. Professor Liegey was an excellent teacher who had, I believe, eleven or so children. He encouraged me to read and write. He was very pleased with one composition I wrote and he gave an A-. I had written about life in Puerto Rico, how I hadn't seen tall buildings nor gone to a beach and what it was like coming as a hillbilly from the country and being faced with life in the City.

It is because I developed such an interest in these writers and poets, that I began to read biographies on my own at the Aguilar Library at 110th Street and Lexington Ave. I was especially interested in the love letters of Keats, Shelly, Donne and the works of Poe. This was my first real exposure to English literature, since I had not received much instruction in this area in high school. Later I developed an interest in Spanish literature and poetry and learned that we had literary figures who were the equal of the great English poets and writers, in Spain, Latin America

and Puerto Rico. There were poets such as Pablo
Neruda, Rubén Darío, Gabriela Mistral, Luís Lloréns
Torres, and Luis Pales Matos and authors such as
Gabriel García Marquez, Carlos Fuentes and José
Martí. I learned as much as I could about Latin
American poetry; I became a great fan of Pablo
Neruda, and became very familiar with his work,
which includes, "Los Versos del Capitán", (the
Verses of the Captain), Twenty Poems of Love, and
his other works. I also very much enjoyed, "Alturas
de América" (Highlights of America), written by Luís
Llorens Torres, a Puerto Rican poet, lawyer and
great orator. I enjoyed, in particular "La Palma
Bruja", "La Hija del Viejo Pancho" (The Daughter of
Old Man Pancho) and one that became my favorite
"El Valle de Collores" (The Valley of Collores). I
grew to love this literature so much that later in my
life, when I became Assistant to the Mayor, I went
to New York University and audited courses in
Spanish and Latin American Literature and Poetry.

When I returned to Fordham in 1947, after
being discharged from the Navy, the students in my
class were mostly G.I.s who had been in the Second
World War. I still lived on Lexington Avenue and I
met a whole group of Italian friends at Fordham,
among them, Al Fiorella, who came from 116th Street
and Park Avenue. Fiore Terraciano, whose parents
owned a drug store was also from East Harlem and

Ray Leonardo from Mount Vernon. It was kind of comical because we behaved just like the girls. Fordham had sister schools, namely Manhattanville, Mount St. Vincent and Marymount, in Tarrytown. These were the Catholic equivalent of the Ivy League women's colleges. The schools would organize socials and the white Fordham students would decide who could attend and would send the name of those students. The school having the social would have a list and when you got there you would be presented, your name would be read off and you would be paired off with whatever young lady would be your date. When we met the girls, we would leave to go to the john together to compare notes.

On one occasion, I was paired with a girl named Alice Lavec from St. Vincent's. My friend, Al Fiorella, mentioned that I lived on Park Avenue, because they would not know that Park Avenue and 116th Street was Spanish Harlem. Terraciano had a 1941 Buick, which was supposed to be a big deal. My friends urged me to tell the girl that we had a car and to ask if she wanted to go for a ride. When I finally did, she asked me what kind of car we had and I said we had a '41 Buick. She replied, "I ride in nothing less than Cadillacs", a comment that generated a great deal of amusement when I met my friends in the john.

While at Fordham, when I was approaching the age of eighteen, World War II was raging. This was in 1945, and I was worried about being drafted into the Army and going to the Infantry. I much preferred the Navy and started looking into enlisting. I attempted to enlist in the Coast Guard but I couldn't because, lo and behold, I found out that I did not have a birth certificate. It turns out that my birth certificate was lost when the church in my hometown was wiped out by San Felipe, one of the storms that ravaged Puerto Rico. Also, I was under eighteen so I needed my parents' consent. About five days before my eighteenth birthday, which was on August 21, 1945, I enlisted in the Navy with the aid of my mother who listed my father as dead. When I left for the Navy, I was a sophomore at Fordham going into the junior year. When I started as a freshman, there were twenty-five students. When I left there were only nine in my class because they were too young to be in the service. Most of the students were away fighting World War II. Although I joined five days before my eighteenth birthday, I was not called into the Navy until October 1945. I would have used those two months at home to complete another term at school and would have been a junior.

Chapter Five
The Service

The Navy sent me to boot camp at Camp Peary, Virginia, a camp that had been used to house prisoners of war. I was in a company of 120 men and we underwent a grueling course of training. Camp Peary was a primitive place. We were only allowed to have one set of dirty clothes at a time. We washed them in the showers, but there weren't enough showers nor hot water, so often we washed our clothes under cold water. Each barracks had forty to sixty men. They were heated with cannon ball stoves that had to be fed coal constantly. When they were hot, the barracks were stifling. If the fire went out and the stove got cold, then you would freeze. The person on guard duty was assigned to take care of the stoves and on one occasion when someone let the stove get cold, I got very sick. I contracted a terrible cold and wound up in the hospital with catarrhal fever; something that I think still plagues me to this day. Although, as a pre-med student, I was in a hospital training school, when you reported on sick leave and went to the clinic, no matter how sick you were, you were given two "APC" pills, all-purpose cures.

There were very few guys from New York in my company. For the first time in my life, I was thrown in with people from the South and from all areas of the country. There were no Puerto Ricans or Latinos. The only person in my company whom I knew was Vincent "Red" Scully, a guy from Fordham. He would later become a baseball announcer for the Brooklyn Dodgers and is now in the Hall of Fame. Another classmate of mine from Fordham, whom I did not know at the time, was Francis Murphy. When I first became a judge, Murphy was the Chief Judge of the Appellate Division. His father was a political leader and he made his son a judge as soon as he graduated from law school. I also befriended, Pasqual D'Ambrosio, a fellow from West New York, who was Italian.

We received all of our training at Camp Peary and did not get leave the entire time we were there.

John - Water - Army

When basic training was over, I thought I would be sent to China or the Far East. I was, in fact, shipped to the U.S. Naval Hospital Corps School Program in San Diego, California where I would study to be a hospital apprentice. The Navy decided they would send me to the medical program to be a hospital corpsman. The program was at the San Diego Naval Hospital and lasted six to eight weeks. My class at the San Diego Hospital was made up of pre-medical students from all over the United States. It was the middle of the war and there were many casualties coming from the Pacific, as well as from Europe. It took five days by train to travel to San Diego from Camp Peary, Virginia.

Our train seemed to be twice the length of a normal train, so I traveled with a great number of men in close quarters. I was exposed to whatever viruses such a big group of people invariably carry. Getting sick on the trip meant a lot of discomfort. There was an incidence of diarrhea that proved to be a really big problem because there were just not enough toilets on the train. Illness aside, the trip was uneventful, except for one instance of group "mooning" of a town we passed along the way.

Rudy Zapata and I with our Mothers

The men at the Hospital Corps School were mostly college kids and came from all parts of the country. Many joined the Medical Corps because they planned to be doctors. We were training to be "hospital apprentices," although I soon learned that that was the polite word for what we were. In Navy language we were called "pecker checkers" or "peter machinists." Again, there were no Latinos in my group, no Puerto Ricans and I ended up hanging out with four young sailors, Frank DeJoy, Moya, Perry and Blair Vernon Anderson, who was a Mormon from Salt Lake City, Utah. Moya and

DeJoy were from Pueblo, Colorado. Among them, Dejoy is one of the few I remained in contact with after the war. Years later he would come to visit me in New York. My friends and I were like Musketeers. We joined the boxing team because it meant we wouldn't have to take physical education. Besides, when you fought, you got a day off the next day, and that made us feel like special people.

Hospital corpsmen were trained by working in the wards: giving inoculations, injections, handling the pharmacology and, generally learning what it was like to work in a hospital. I enjoyed the work and fully intended to enter medicine after completing my service. Class was very competitive and we were tested on what we learned. I ended up number three in the class based on my grade performance on tests, but I did have two problems. One was that, to graduate, you had to practice injecting each other in the arm, but I had developed an aversion to needles. I couldn't stand them. I guess I saw too many people passing out when they got shots. I just refused to do it. The administration learned of this and I was ordered to go see the Head Nurse who was in charge of the program. She told me in no uncertain terms, that I had to get over this fear. If I did not practice giving shots with other corpsmen, I would not pass the course. The day that I went to see her I had two friends sitting outside the office. It took some effort on her part to help me get over my fear. She began by explaining to me that we should practice, I would give her an injection and then she would inject me. I was still reluctant and she hollered at me, "Give it to me, John, give it to me!" My fellow swabbies were outside during the whole exchange but they did not know what this was about. They chose to misinterpret what they heard and yelled, "Give it to her John, for crying out loud, give it to her!" I managed to give it to her, that is, the injection, and got over the hurdle in time to graduate with the third highest average in the class.

When we finished the course, I was surprised to learn that I would not ship out to China or the

Pacific, from where a lot of the injured servicemen were coming, but instead my shipping orders called for me to go to Treasure Island Naval Hospital, which was at the base of the Oakland Bay Bridge, between Oakland and San Francisco. I was a little unhappy at the time. This is where I would spend the rest of my time in the Navy. My only sea duty would be on shore leave and taking the ferry over from Treasure Island to San Francisco. It wasn't as bad as I thought it would be and Treasure Island turned out to be a wonderful place to work and get experience. The Oakland Bay Bridge is seven and a quarter miles long and the hospital was located at the base of that small island. The hospital was large and functioned as a feeder for several other hospitals. It was crowded and there was lots of work to be done, so I received all kinds of experiences: in dirty surgery, clean surgery, orthopedics, operating rooms, ward work and the like and it was fascinating to me. I did manage to make Hospital Apprentice, First Class.

The work was fine and there was little controversy during my time in San Diego, except once. The services were not integrated as of yet and would not be until 1948. At one point we received two young black sailors who were college men and had been assigned to train at the hospital to be corpsmen. No one stationed there would room with them. I volunteered to have them bunk with me. I had not been exposed to this kind of racism and in fact had lived with and gone to school with black people. Some of my colleagues, many of whom were from the South, weren't too happy with my decision. They started calling me a "N- lover," but that kind of conduct did not affect me. They were both fine young men who I am sure had gone back to college and became excellent doctors.

Working in the hospital meant that we had our dining room to provide our meals. We didn't have to go elsewhere for food and I went up from 123 lbs. to 145 lbs. I was eating as many as six eggs in the morning for breakfast and eating all kinds of food. I was worried about how much I was eating and whether I would continue to overeat when I got home. I was also concerned about the amount of cursing, since every conversation was peppered with "F-" this or "F-" that.

Although I enjoyed my work, I never got to enjoy San Francisco. I was only nineteen at the time and in California in those days, the drinking age was twenty-one. Not being able to drink was not a problem for me, but because I was underage I could not go to many places such as nightclubs. Not only that, but in California then everything stopped at midnight. If you were out after 12:00 midnight, the subways and buses had stopped running, and it was very difficult to get back to the base. We had no transportation, no cars of our own. You had to make sure that before you went out on leave, you arranged for taxis and / or whatever cars were available or you would not be able to get back in time. Hence, I did not get to experience or see that famous nightlife that San Francisco's known for. I did go out during the day and I visited Japan Town, China Town and the Mexican neighborhoods there and off the coast, on the other side of the Golden Gate Bridge. I went to Fisherman's Wharf and ate at a couple of restaurants. I also did get to visit the John Muir Woods and see the redwoods, but never made it to Carmel, Monterrey or Sausalito.

USNR Boot Camp Circa 1945

One opportunity I availed myself of was to attend football games when I volunteered to take injured servicemen to the games. At the time, the San Francisco Forty-niners were the big team, with Frankie Albert as the quarter back and Herman "Hula Hoop" Widemeyer, who were among the football greats of the time. I went to many games at Kezar Stadium, wheeling servicemen in and sitting on the fifty-yard line. I was too young to appreciate the beauty of San Francisco. It was only many years later that I really got to know San Francisco and its environs. In fact, if I had been a federal judge, I would have liked to have been transferred there, since San Francisco became my favorite city in the United States.

I wrote home often. I wrote to my girlfriend, Terry, daily. My record was writing her ten letters in one day of ten pages each. Beyond work in the hospital, there was little else to do but to write home. My time in the service felt like jail time. I was told when to go to bed, when to get up and what to do in between. I had been taken away from what I wanted to do; to go back, finish college and go on to medical school. Other sailors and servicemen, particularly Southerners, "Rebels", seemed to enjoy life and the food in the service. They liked being away from home. They liked the

life enough to remain as career servicemen. I
missed my home and my freedom.

Working in a hospital was another story. I
enjoyed the experience of making the calls with the
doctors in the mornings and on the weekends. We
entertained ourselves with practical jokes. On
weekend visiting days, for example, we would get
100 cc glass tubes, fill them with tomato juice and
cruise up and down the hall spraying juice up in the
air and catching it in my mouth. We relished
making people think that the corpsmen were
horrible. Even many of the servicemen, who were
patients, were in on the jokes. When we went into
the wards, they would scream as if we were doing
horrific acts, much to the dismay of visitors.

The most harrowing day of my time in
hospital corps was the day I volunteered for
ambulance duty on New Year's Eve on Market
Street. Market Street was like Times Square in New
York. There were two of us who volunteered for
ambulance duty that night and we were ordered to
report at six o'clock to a local hospital in the center
of the city. Things seemed to be routine enough
until about six or seven o'clock when things started
happening. There were only two doctors in
attendance. By the time ten or eleven rolled
around, the accidents were piling up and we were

doing run after run in the ambulance. On one run to the scene of a terrible auto accident, I remember having to put the severed leg of one of the victims onto a stretcher. By midnight at the hospital all hell had broken loose. I was pumping stomachs, working on patients who needed brain surgery, amputations and any number of horrendous things; procedures that were the work of doctors but there were not enough doctors to be found. By seven a.m. we were exhausted. That terrible night in San Francisco taught me never to go out on New Year's Eve again. It seemed to be a time that brought out the worst in people. The depression and drinking resulted in so many attempted suicides that we didn't have enough ambulances to get to everyone who needed help.

It was during my time in the Navy that I first learned about sex. I served with a young sailor who was a patient in the hospital and was able to visit with his wife. He began telling me about his sex life, which made me begin to wonder about the things I had never done. I decided that it was time for me to have a sex life as well. I did not act on my decision until the week before I was being discharged, when I went out with three other sailors, Glass, Kaufman and Testasica, determined to lose our virginity on Market Street. On that night, my friends and I managed to solicit a cabdriver who said he would get us the services of a prostitute for twenty-five dollars each. We chipped in our moneys and he engaged one hooker to for all of us, which meant we had to take turns. We were very naïve and the entire episode was pretty funny. As one of my buddies, Kaufman, was going in to take his turn, he called out to me, "Carro, Carro." I went thinking something had happened to him, but when I asked what was wrong it turned out he had an important question, "when do I come?" For our twenty-five dollars each, our sessions lasted all of two or three minutes. I decided to get more for my money and when my turn came, I tried to slow things down. I had never closely observed a woman's anatomy and I spent so much time examining the prostitute that she concluded that I was a little weird. We were all pretty excited about our adventure except we began to worry that we had contracted some venereal disease. We had one week left before we were discharged and during that time we gave each other penicillin shots and worried a great deal every time we urinated.

I have always regretted that I saw so little of San Francisco during my time there as a sailor. I made an ill-fated attempt to connect with the Mexican community by attending a dance. I thought that I would be warmly received by my fellow Latinos because we had shared a lot in common. I went to the dance with Rudy Zapata, a friend of mine in the service, who had come from New York to visit. We were not welcomed at all, in fact, they did not know what Puerto Ricans were or where Puerto Ricans came from. This was a time when Mexicans were trying hard to assimilate. They did not want to identify with their cultural background and they decidedly did not want to speak Spanish. For my part, I was completely unaware of the history of violence between young Mexican Americans and servicemen that resulted in the Zoot-Suit Riots of the early '40's,[8] which probably accounted for the less than friendly reception.

---

[8] The riots took place in 1942 and 1943 in Los Angeles. They were sparked by the arrest and conviction of seventeen young Mexican American men for the murder of another young Mexican American. The defendants were arrested in massive sweep of the city carried out by 600 police officers. During the ensuing riots, sailors in uniforms cruised the streets using makeshift weapons. The zoot suit was a mode of dress that expressed rejection of traditional ways. It was much despised by the authorities who attempted to outlaw it in a number of ways. The convictions were eventually overturned. American Experience: The Zoot Suit Riots, PBS/WGBH, Boston.

Chapter Six
Home Again

I was discharged from the Navy on January 24, 1947. Under the G.I. Bill, I would receive $52.00 a month, for about twenty months under the G.I. bill. I was in a hurry to make up for the two years I spent in the service. Terry and I had maintained a correspondence throughout my time away. I had no time for a long courtship. We were married about six months after I was discharged from the Navy. The wedding was a simple one; a Catholic ceremony in St. John's Chrysostom, a church on 167th Street in the Bronx. We had two receptions: a small reception at my mother's apartment, where liquor was served and another at my wife's apartment, where coffee and cake was served. My best man was a friend, Rudy Zapata and Terry's brother, Alfred, attended along with members of my family. I gave my wife a wedding ring I bought for $150 at Gray Rudder's in East Harlem.

We had a honeymoon of sorts. First we stayed at the home of Terry's friend, Mary Flores, in Midland Beach, Staten Island. That did not work out well, and after two days, we went camping in Bear Mountain and Lake Tiorati. This proved to be very difficult. There were no powdered meals in those days, so I took along a backpack that weighed over fifty pounds because it was filled with cans of food. It wasn't long before we grew tired of hiking and after one day at a campsite, we decided to chuck the entire adventure. Neither Terry nor I liked sleeping on the ground anymore than we enjoyed hiking. To make matters worse, I invited my cousin, Charlie Torres, who was like a kid brother, to come along with us. It was a short-lived honeymoon and within a week we were back home in my mother's apartment, where I would return to my studies.

I was able to get back into Fordham in February, a week after my discharge and enrolled in the class of 1949. In this class there was a bumper crop. Many returning veterans were anxious to exercise their GI bill of rights and I was one of those who joined the 52-20 club. Fordham still had few Latinos or blacks. The friends I went to school with included Al Fiorella who lived on 116th Street and Park Avenue, and Terry Terraciano, Ralph Leonardo and Mike Fumarola. I now lived on 164th St. and Prospect Avenue in the Bronx and I commuted by bus to Fordham University. Fordham was a Jesuit school and in my religion class we were taught by Father Mulqueen who was well known in the school because he had a habit of insulting students who asked what he considered asinine questions. One day in class, when he was speaking about G-d being all just, I somehow said that I had some question about G-d's justice in the sense that if I as a Catholic committed a mortal sin, forgot to confess and died with a mortal sin on my soul, I would go to hell. On the other hand if someone like Stalin, who murdered thousands of people, managed to convert and confess, he would be absolved of his sins, he would possibly not suffer the same fate as I. I could not see the justice in that. When Father Mulqueen heard this, he became so incensed that he leaped up in the air and landed on the desk. He proceeded to call me every name in the book, you pimple on the rump of Providence, you @ss hole, you carbuncle on the @ss. He had done this before with several students and I saw how they had been totally humiliated. While he was doing this, I got up and told him, "You're lucky I'm a Catholic because if I were not, I would have left the faith long ago. I have never been insulted and humiliated in this manner in front of my classmates. When I started remonstrating with him, he quieted down and we had a recess during which he apologized to me. It was odd, because up to that point, I was about a 75% student in class, but after that incident, because I had the audacity to stop his insults, I became a 90% student.

At another time in Father Mulqueen's class there was an incident involving Johnny Bach, a star player on our basketball team, along with Jerry Smith and several others. We sat together at the back of the classroom because he was Bach and I was Carro and we would talk about the previous week's basketball game. I was talking in class, when Father Mulqueen looked up and said "Carro, one thousand lines, you're old enough to have better sense." I thought it was ridiculous, looked at him and laughed but he seemed to be for real. A week later it was up to 7000 lines then 10,000 lines. He said to me, "Listen, if you don't have these 10,000 lines you are not going to pass this course. Now, if you want to do something about it, come and see me." I certainly did not want to write 10,000 lines. I felt that was rather immature, so I decided to go see him instead. In his quarters, he said I had a choice: either do the 10,000 lines or select an alternative. When I asked about the alternative, he open a drawer and showed me a drumstick, a ruler and several other items. He said that in lieu of the 10,000 lines I could get twelve whacks in the @ss and asked me to drop my pants. This put me in a quandary. Here I was a veteran, GI from the Second World War, a college man in his twenties with a wife and child and here was this priest asking me to drop my pants and get twelve whacks in the @ss. However, I learned in the service that discretion was the better part of valor and it was either submit to this or flunk the course. I had no intention of flunking and decided that I would take my remedy. I dropped my pants; he put me across his lap and proceeded to whack me twelve times. To add insult to injury, he asked me if it hurt and I wanted to say "you bet it does, you son-of-a-bitch," but I took my medicine. Strangely enough, Father Mulqueen was elected by my graduating class as the most popular teacher in the school.

I was now married and to help me pay for the expenses I shared with my mother, I joined the ROTC at Fordham, which meant that once I graduated, I would become a lieutenant. This provided me with pay of $25 per month, which, along with the $100 or so I received allowed me to help my mother pay for rent and food. The rent was $48 a month and after paying my share, I was left with about $100 to pay for food for me, my wife and our daughter Sherry, who was born in December, 1947.

As participants in ROTC, we had classes weekly and drills once per week at 42th Street and 11th Ave. I became attached to the 470th AAA Gun Battalion, an outfit that was made up of many ROTC members and some discharged GI's. In addition to the weekly drills and instruction, every summer from 1949 to 1954, we would have a two-week session during which the outfit would be sent to Camp Edwards in Provincetown Massachusetts for summer training. While at Camp Edwards, I had occasion to get to know Cape Cod and to visit Hyannis and the surrounding area. It is a very nice place in New England that I had never seen. At the end of 1949, when I graduated from Fordham, I was commissioned as a first lieutenant in the US Army Reserve. I continued in the Reserve from 1949 until 1954, when I began attending law school.

In 1954, we were close to entering the Korean War and they were beginning to draft and send Reserve outfits to Korea. I had a choice of staying in the ROTC and possibly be drafted. If I stayed in the ROTC I would qualify for a pension after twenty years and who knows how high I would have reached. In 1954, I was ready to be promoted to captain. However, I chose to enter Brooklyn Law School, which I attended from 1954 to 1956. I sought a discharge from ROTC to attend law school and I was discharged as a first lieutenant after five years in the Reserve.

My experience in ROTC was good. In addition to two summers at Camp Edwards, I attended a six-week course at Fort Bragg prior to being commissioned as an officer. That experience was an excellent one. I was put in charge of a unit, the 470th AAA Gun Battalion that was made up mostly of African American troops. They treated me royally, as "Good Ole Lieutenant Carro" and I got along well with the men. After the ROTC, I still had my ID. When I went on vacation to Puerto Rico with my family, there were military installations at which I had privileges as a World War II veteran. I could go to the PX and purchase clothes and liquor. I was also able to use some of the bases that had excellent beaches. I went to a beach on the outskirts of San Juan that was run by the Navy and I had an incident that sticks in my mind. I went swimming there one day and while diving under water, I saw what appeared to be rock. When I stepped on it, it turned out to be a sea urchin, which is like a porcupine and I wound up with about thirty needles embedded in my foot. For a minute I thought that my vacation was over as my leg swelled up. However, when I went to my Aunt Amparo's house in Bayamon, I discovered that Puerto Ricans have an antidote called *sebo flande*, cow's utter, that you rub on it. She managed to get some, rubbed it on my leg, bandaged it and, lo and behold, the next day the swelling had subsided and the spikes that had embedded in my foot and ankle came out. It was wonderful since I thought that I would be laid up for three weeks. I missed the ROTC, but I was glad to be in law school and busy trying to get a legal education.

Upon my return from the service, I also felt a great deal of pressure to finish college and to go on to medical school. I couldn't work full-time while going to college, so I spent much of my time studying at the Aguilar Library at 110th Street and Lexington Avenue, as it turned out, one of the librarians, Esther Bonilla, was the sister of the man who would become my lifelong friend, Frank Bonilla. I often did my homework there and did a great deal of reading. During the week I was able to immerse myself in the things that most interested me; literature and poetry. I read the work and biographies of poets such as Edgar Allan Poe, Keats, Shelly and Dunne. I studied all week and on the weekends I went dancing with Terry to the Palladium Dance Hall at 53rd Street and Broadway where Latin bands, such as, Machito, Tito Puente, Tito Rodriguez and Vincente Valdez, would play. Sometimes there would be dance contests and well-known Latino dancers such as Augie and Margo and Pete and Milly would perform.

This was the era when Latin dance scene attracted people, not just Latinos but Italians and Jews. It was the time of the Mambo and often celebrities and movie stars, like Marlon Brando, would show up at the Palladium. On Saturdays, we generally went to the Hotel Diplomat, where the Latin dances were sponsored by the person who would turn out to be law clerk for Judge Manny Gomez. Sometimes I would work part-time to earn a little money to buy clothes, haircuts and pay for the movies. I did a stint as a tray boy, working from 6 pm to 10pm, at Toots Shore's, famous restaurant in Rockefeller Center. My job as a tray boy was one step below that of a bus boy. I would load up trays of dishes in the dining room until they were full, and then took them downstairs. I loved my job at Toots Shore's because the restaurant was frequented by movie stars and sports figures and luminaries such Joe DiMaggio, Mel Ott, Billy Conn, Jimmy Durante, Frank Sinatra. There were glamorous movie stars like Lana Turner and Ava Gardner and I was exhilarated just being in their presence. One day I loaded a tray with the dishes from Lana Turner's table. She left part of the steak on her plate and I proceeded to take home and show Mom and everybody the steak that Lana Turner had bitten into.

While I was living with my mother at 1083 Lexington Avenue and 111th Street, she found a furnished apartment for sale at 850 E. 164th Street in the Bronx that we purchased for $1400. It had three bedrooms, a parlor and a kitchen. I had never lived in the Bronx, but this was certainly better than living in a furnished room in El Barrio. We managed to scrape together the $1400 and considered ourselves lucky to have a place to live. Rent was $52.00 a month and I agreed that I would pay the rent and help with the food. By this time, Terry and I had a baby, our daughter Sherry Lynn, and we lived on Prospect Avenue for three years until we were able to get our own apartment on 1312 Rosedale Avenue in the Bronx. While living with my mother, Terry became fluent in Spanish and learned Puerto Rican cooking, although she burned the beans a few times.

Once again, my mother, proved to be the pioneer in the family. She had saved the money from her earnings to buy an apartment while she was still a sewing machine operator. Because we had three bedrooms, many of our relatives who came to the United States lived with us. This included my Uncle Luís who came and stayed with us before he went to the Civilian Conservation Corps camp. Then my Aunt Carmen came there with her kids, her brother Berto plus several friends such as Sophie, and Victor Colón who subsequently became a dentist and married Carmen. My mother gave them and many others an initial foothold in the U.S. This was a rough time in our history. It was during the Korean War and jobs were not plentiful.

The economy was in a recession and there were many Puerto Ricans were coming from the Island, looking for work. The numbers swelled to about 600,000, at a time when not only jobs but also housing were hard to get.

I was anxious to help my mother with finances. The first job I was able to get upon graduation from Fordham, was in a place called Clark's Clothes on 125th Street in Harlem. My title was something like "credit manager." I had no idea what that meant, but they told to use the name "Mr. Francis" and call people who were behind in their accounts to remind them they owed money. I soon found that I was given a phony name, because invariable irate customers would come in looking for the person who had been calling them at home about their debts.

I only lasted a week at that job and the next thing that came along was a job at the White Castle hamburger place at 46th Street and Eighth Avenue, working nights from 12:00 midnight to 8:00 are. It did not pay much money, maybe fifty to sixty dollars a week, but I needed to work. My mother was devastated. She had struggled to send me to college, I earned a B.S., but instead of going to medical school, I was making hamburgers for a living and didn't even know how to do that very well, even though I was given a three-day learning course on how to make hamburgers and cheeseburgers. The White Castle was located in an area that was full of prostitutes and vagrants. It wasn't quite the place to go. My mother was incensed. She told me, "Look, I didn't send you to college to do this kind of work. Even if this is the only job you can get, I would rather you quit." Fortunately, a week later I read in the papers that the Department of Welfare, Social Services it was called, was appointing fifty provisional workers to handle a burgeoning workload.

I applied and was one of the fifty selected to a "provisional" position, which meant that you did not have to take the Civil Service exam to be hired. Because of the need for services to the Puerto Rican and Latino community, you were required to speak Spanish. There was a ceremony that was attended by the Commissioner of Welfare, Raymond Hilliard, as well as one of the two Puerto Ricans then serving in the City administration, Manuel Gómez, who had some sort of city job. The other Puerto Rican official who was not present was José Ramos López. Gómez, who subsequently became the first Puerto Rican criminal court judge in New York City, made quite an impression on me that day because he wore ice cream colored socks.

In the group of fifty appointees, there were people who would become my friends for life. Among them, Frank Bonilla, who became my dearest friend, was also married and needed work. He had just finished attending City College. There was Antonio Figueroa, (Tony), who also was looking for work out of college and who would eventually become a criminal court judge. Many other people I would come to know, such as Carmen Aponte, Leon Brown, Carlos Plaud and Joe Barreras, the basketball player for St. John's, were among that class of fifty Latino hires. Frank, Tony, Joe and I were assigned to work at the Melrose Welfare Center on 161st Street in the Bronx.

The salary was a little over $2900 and the job was to review the eligibility of people to receive public assistance and to supervise a caseload of seventy-five to a hundred people who require monthly visits. During the visits, we checked on living arrangements and determined the needs of people on our caseloads. I was initially assigned to a unit supervisor named Miss Ethel Cherry, who was a well-meaning, nerdy type of person. Others in my unit were Archibald Purvis an old timer who had many years of experience. Frank and Tony were assigned to other units in the Melrose Center in the Bronx. Working for the Department of Welfare was much better than working at Clark's or White

Castle, but it was not where I saw myself in the future. I had a family and I was still unsure what I was going to do in life. I had not gotten into medical school and was trying to decide whether I would pursue a master's in biology, to increase my chances of getting admitted. Even if I got in, I did not know how I would support my family during the four or five years I would be attending medical school.

I made many friends in the Bronx, among them, Frank Bonilla, Rustam Sharir, Charlie Jímenez, Bob García, John Sylvia, Mae Santiago and Skip Moret. They were part of a group of WWII veterans we assembled, in an attempt to get an American Legion charter. We first tried to get an American Legion charter but were turned down and told that we would have to join the American Legion Charter at 162nd Street and Prospect Avenue. We wanted our own charter and began to scout around. We founded a group called the American Veteran's Committee headed by Shenley Egeth and Bernie Belush. Shirley Egeth subsequently became a judge and Bernie Belush was a City College professor. They agreed to be sponsors for our own American Veteran's Committee Chapter.

My friends and I also established a social club. "The Rovallies" which became a weekend gathering place under the direction of Frank and me. The name Rovallies came from the words "Rovers and Allies." We held square dances, and organized weekend outings, birthday celebrations, Halloween parties and Thanksgiving parties. We even went as far as producing a play, which Frank Bonilla wrote about the Rovallies in the year 1975. At the time, we would spend weekends at the Spanish Villas up in the Catskill Mountains, Route 32, where there were a series of Spanish villas: Villa García, Villa Pérez, Villa Nueva and Villa Rodriguez. We also went on outings to Jones Beach and Robert Moses State Park, as well as, the local beach, Orchard Beach, in the Bronx.

At the time of the Rovallies, Frank and I both worked at the Melrose Welfare Center on 161st and Melrose Avenue as social investigators. Frank was attending City College while I attended Fordham. My friendship with Frank, who lived nearby, at Tiffany Street at #932 and while we lived at #866, blossomed and we would often visit each other's families. Terry would cook empanadas, bacalaítos, arroz con tocino, fried chicken and Frank's mother would make alcapurrias and other great dishes. We lived half a block away in a four room apartment; two bedrooms above the Union Bar. Angelo Cintrón and his wife Norma and their children, Mike, Richie and Barbara, were friends who lived nearby on Southern Boulevard and became our compadres.

One night at the Rovallies Social Club a fight broke out at about 2:00 or 3:00 in the morning when one of the local groups from Rickie's Bar, Abie, Lefty, Gordo and his friends, pushed their way into our club and we were compelled to ask them to leave. They would not leave and challenged us to a fight. Since I was the President, I was elected to represent the Rovallies and the other side selected Lefty. The fight had a referee, Detective Richard Texeira, "Tex", a local detective who was well known by everybody. Before we went downstairs, Frank volunteered to take my place. The group laughed and told him, "Put your glasses back on." It was 3:00 in the morning and Lefty and I were to have a fair fight. He struck me first, on the side of the head with his fist and I went down twice. I struck him on the side of the head and sprained my wrist. I was knocked down and stomped on by the group. Three days later, when I was well enough to renew the fight, I looked up Lefty at Rickie's Bar and offered to finish the fight. He apologized for the fact that I was stomped by his friends and said that we would have no more trouble from them. We became friends thereafter.

I found that I loved working with people. When I first went to work at Welfare in the Bronx, I was given a caseload of mostly old people, Jewish people all of whom lived in one area, Fox Street and Simpson Street. In fact, my entire caseload could be found in a couple of buildings on Fox Street that were rooming houses. They were railroad type apartments, with one bathroom for four or five rooms and the landlords were, in effect, ripping off the old people who had few, if any, relatives. They were in dire need and looked forward to our visits. They were also very kind and it really broke my heart to see that they needed coats and shoes and had many medical problems.

We did whatever we could to help them, but the bureaucracy got in the way. To get them a warm sweater or anything else they needed, you had to get a requisition from the case supervisor, then go to the unit supervisor and on and on before it was approved. Sometimes, so much time elapsed that the weather changed by the time you got them the item. It was a very frustrating job. We were required to visit each of the families at least once a month, but some of the old-time case workers I worked with just did not do their jobs serving the people on their caseloads. Meanwhile, I visited everyone on my caseload during the first two weeks of the month and the second two weeks were meant for completing paperwork. Instead, I found I was also expected to do the work of others, who had not made their visits. This added as many as fifty visits to my workload. Many of my co-workers just didn't seem to care very much about their poor clients.

There were other problems with the job. I had not been assigned to work with Puerto Ricans or Latinos, which was one of the reasons I went to work for the Department of Welfare. Then, there was the policy of making provisional appointments creating a discriminatory system. As a provisional, I had to take and pass a civil service exam to become a permanent, full-time worker. I had to work a full year to qualify to take the test, but provisional assignments were given only nine months credit. I could not join the union and I didn't receive the raises given to civil service employees. I could only progress in my job if I got a master's degree in social work. Unfortunately, in New York there were two graduate schools of social work, Hunter and Columbia, and both required that you attend full-time during the day, something I could not do and support my family. I worked at Welfare Department from 1949 to 1952.

I began to look for work that offered some advancement and more money. I found an opening as a probation officer in the Children's Court, which was located at 167th Street and the Grand Concourse in the Bronx. As a probation officer, I would work with children under sixteen who needed supervision because they were abused or neglected or who had committed juvenile crimes.

I was hired as a provisional probation officer in Children's Court and placed under the supervision of Elizabeth Corning. I was very fortunate to have Ms. Corning as a supervisor because it was she who gave the grounding, education and experience to become a good probation officer and to do an outstanding and thorough job. She reviewed my work in investigating the situation of the children who were brought before the Court and guided me in determining the intervention that was needed. Many had school problems and were Persons In Need of Supervision, "PINS". They were neglected children and my job was to report to the Court with recommendations for what services they should receive, such as treatment, supervision, referral, placement, and working with parents. The children were under the age of sixteen and had committed crimes when they were between the ages of seven and sixteen. Children who committed serious felonies, such as murder, could be treated as juveniles, or as adults, and there were serious consequences as to which category you were placed. As a juvenile, your case was adjudicated in Children's Court and you could be sentenced to serve no more than sixteen months, or until you were twenty-one. As an adult, you would be tried for felony murder for which you could get life imprisonment in the adult system and little treatment, if any.

The juvenile probation system had its own problems. First, there was the fact of segregation by religion. Catholic children who were PINS went to Lincoln Hall. If you were Jewish it was Hawthorne Cedar Knolls. If you were Protestant, it was the Wittwick School for boys. Those with more serious problems went to Children's Village. Those who had committed the most serious crimes went to the Warwick State Training School. Not everyone was sent away and you could make referrals to agencies that worked with the system without having to place the child. Even having a probation officer who was competent and experienced did not guarantee that the best interests of the child would be advanced. The judges who presided in Children's Court were political Mayoral appointees. They usually were cronies of the Mayor, who were only interested in being named judges. Many of them had no interest in juveniles and only concerned themselves with getting promotions. A few of the judges merited their appointments, among them Justine Weiss Polier, Justice Jane Bolin and Leonard Ruisi, but many of the rest were political hacks who had no real interest in youths and their problems. One judge who was Catholic, Justice Fogarty, his only interest was whether the child knew that the Fifth Commandment said "thou shall not kill." If he asked you that question and you knew the answer he would send you to Lincoln Hall. Then there was Judge McCaffrey, whose only interest was in baseball, Judge Delaney, who was African American, did not believe in psychiatric help for minorities or Judge Kaplan who believed that juveniles were amoral. There were judges like Wilfred Waltermade, who believed that incarceration or punishment was what was called for in most cases.

In this system, the judge was judge, jury and prosecutor in the case and your job as probation officer was only to give a report or make a recommendation that the judge could accept or deny. The judges were free to do pretty much what they pleased with the children. If a child was sent to an institution for fourteen to sixteen months, then he stood a chance. Generally speaking there were so many juveniles who came before the court, that many were simply put on probation. There were far too few probation officers who could give them the kind of supervision and help that they needed. Some agencies, such as JSA, Jewish Service Agency, took an interest in helping the court, but very few agencies were available to Catholics or Protestants.

As a whole, there were not enough ancillary services to give the help these young, troubled people required.

In the court itself, which was closed to the public, the rules of evidence did not apply or were not adhered to. The probation officer would report on the case and the court generally followed the recommendations. The defendants generally had no attorney to represent them and no attorneys were assigned, so things were pretty much in the hands of the judge. There were no assistant district attorneys available to prosecute the child and it was a catch-as-catch-can situation where everything depended on the particular probation officer assigned to the case. There was the example of the Puerto Rican youth who was alleged to have killed another youth with a zip gun, although the likelihood was that the shooting may have been an accident. The Judge who presided, Wilfred Waltermade, I believed that he was biased against minorities, particularly blacks and Puerto Ricans. When they appeared before him his first instinct was to send them away or to incarcerate them. If he had his way, he would even set bail. I conducted an investigation and I concluded it was not a case of premeditated killing and that the young man merited probation and help. My recommendation was immediately dismissed and the judge said that I should just recommend punishment or incarceration. Although it was difficult, with the help of my supervisor, Elizabeth Corning, I was able have the judge give this kid a break and not put him away. Ms. Corning proved to be, again, an extremely dedicated, experienced woman who always had the best interest of the child in mind.

During my time with the probation office, I had the distinction of being assigned to Lee Harvey Oswald, who was brought to our court as a truant when he was ten or eleven years old. He had been out of school for about 144 days when the Attendance Department had brought him to the court. Oswald lived with his mother, Marguerite Oswald. There was no father at home and he had a brother in the Coast Guard in New York. He was slightly built and spoke with a southern drawl. He was like a duck out of water. His mother had brought him from the South to live in the Bronx, an area that was principally black, Puerto Rican and Jewish. There was no one he could relate to, so he would stay home, go fly pigeons and not bother to go to school. His mother, worked for Hearn's Department Store in the South Bronx and was, at best, well-meaning, but ineffectual and unable to help him. I knew that he needed help, but because he was a Lutheran the only place he could be sent to was the Wiltwyck School, which was used to place largely black children. I spent a year trying to get him help and could not find a placement. I was finally able to get the Protestant Big Brothers to agree to work with him on an outpatient basis, but at this point the mother, Marguerite, did not want to get involved. She said there was no need because he was now going to school, the reason for which he had been placed under court supervision. She felt there was no need for her to be involved in the process. She ignored us and said she wanted to go back home to the South. Although we told her they could not leave the jurisdiction of the court, she proceeded to do just that. Marguerite Oswald never returned to court, so we were not able to help her son and the case was discharged.

Ten years later, on November 26, 1963, Oswald was charged with assassinating President John F. Kennedy. I wasn't even aware of this until I happened to see his mother, Marguerite Oswald on TV. Then I realized that this was the same young man that I had spent a year trying to help in the Children's Court but had not been successful. I was then working as an assistant to Robert Wagner, the Mayor of the City of New York and was attending a meeting of the Police Retirement Board at Police Headquarters when the news of the assassination came. I told the Mayor immediately, since I knew it would be a matter of time before it got out and the media would want to talk to me. I asked the Mayor what I should do and he said just sit tight. Two days later, reporters from the New York Times and Post came to my house for the story. Mayor Wagner gave me permission to go ahead with the interviews. I said what I believed, that had we been able to help in 1953, our history might have been different.

For a while I did not want to be known as the man who had been Oswald's probation officer. I refused to go on the Barry Gray Show, a popular radio show. I did appear on the television show, "To Tell the Truth", with John Daly. No one was able to guess that out of the four participants, who claimed to be Lee Harvey Oswald's probation officer, I was the true one and I won a prize of $400. Aside from that, I chose not to go through life being known as Oswald's probation officer. It was an especially painful in time in my life, because when I was involved in politics and when Jack Kennedy ran for President, I was in charge of his campaign in New York's Latino community, as the head of the Citizen's Committee for the Election of President Kennedy. I had met both him and Jackie and it was hard to imagine how this assassination would change our country. Eleven years later, I testified for three hours before the Warren Commission.[9] Florence Kelly, who was the judge in charge of the court at that time, was not happy. She felt it was a confidential matter and did not want to reveal that we had not been able to help Oswald. In any case, I testified since I had been initially authorized to speak by the Mayor and I believed it was important to have a report of a true record.

In 1954, while still working as a probation officer, I was assigned the case of a young man, fifteen, who killed another person with a zip gun. This was the case that resulted in my decision to become a lawyer. The District Attorney's Office, represented by Burton Roberts, the Bronx County District Attorney, decided that they would allow this matter to be handled as a juvenile offense rather than an adult felony offense. The DA came to Children's Court to drop the criminal charge and let the Children's Court handle it. The young man's family had retained an attorney, José Ramos Lopez, a local politician to appear in the court on behalf of this young man. Although the D.A's Office was ready to drop the case, the

---

[9] The Warren Commission was appointed in 1963 by President Lyndon B. Johnson to investigate the assassination of President John F. Kennedy. The mandate of the Commission was to evaluate the facts surrounding the assassination and the subsequent murder of the alleged assassin, Lee Harvey Oswald by Jack Ruby. The National Archives <archives.gov>

defendant's attorney insisted on getting an adjournment. The prosecutors were justifiably quite angry because they did not want to come back. The DA was so upset that for a while they considered just taking the defendant to Adult Court instead of leaving his case to the Family Court. I asked the family who the attorney was and how did they happen to get him. They said that he was a powerful politician. He had charged them $2500 for the case and they had given him $1000 up front and owed a balance of $1500. It became clear to me the lawyer was getting the adjournment and that he wanted the balance of his money. He had been paid $1000 up front for an appearance and he now wanted another $1500 just to have the young man treated as a juvenile. This attorney did not have the interests of his client as heart. He was getting very close to what I earned in a year for doing harm to this young man. I decided I was on the wrong side of the law. I needed to be in a position where I would be able to help the person charged and the only way I would do so was to be in charge of the case; not as a P.O. but as a defense attorney. So I began to explore going to law school and becoming a lawyer.

THE ROVALLIES SOCIAL CLUB

....young or old....
LET THE GOOD TIMES ROLL!

Chapter Seven
Becoming a Lawyer

I discovered that I could attend law school at night and get a law degree without having to leave my job. Brooklyn Law School was one of the two law schools in New York City that offered night classes. It was a two-year program where you took classes twelve months a year. You attended four nights a week, from six to nine in the evening and summers and you got your law degree. Tuition was $15 a credit and there were no entrance exams required. I called Brooklyn Law School, learned about the requirements and found I was eligible. I applied and a week later, I was accepted for the class of 1954, scheduled to graduate in 1956. I did not have to leave my job, and could commute to Brooklyn from the Bronx by subway. My freshman class at Brooklyn Law School had 125 students, only three of whom were Latino: Luis Garcia, Manuel Ramos and I, and only three women. There was another Latino student, Gilbert Ramirez who was in another class and who was legally blind. A number of people, who would be important in my life, were graduates of Brooklyn Law School. There was Mary Johnston Lowe, who became my law partner, Percy Sutton, who subsequently became Borough President of Manhattan, the future mayor,

David Dinkins, who was my classmate and Herman Badillo who would go into public service and become the Bronx Borough President and Member of Congress from the 22nd District.

While I was at Brooklyn Law School, my friend, Frank Bonilla applied for a John Hay Whitney Opportunity Fellowship, a foundation grant for scholarships available to minority students who had not been able to live up to their potential because of either racial or economic factors. The John Hay Whitney Foundation was headed by Robert Weaver who had been the New York State Rent Administrator under Governor Averill Harriman. It required completing an application, listing all your expenses; household, school and the like; and asking for a scholarship that would cover you for one year. At Frank's urging, I submitted my application for a scholarship to use as a law student and it was granted.

Frank Bonilla was the brightest person I have ever met. He was a star pupil at Morris High School, where Collin Powell attended, and graduated with a 98% average. Frank went on to City College, when it was known for its academics, having awarded more Ph.D.'s than any other college in the nation. Frank graduated cum laude at City College and went on to study at New York

University, where he received a master's degree in one year and to Harvard, where he received his Ph.D. He wrote his dissertation on a study of a generation of Chilean students in South America and developed an expertise in Latin America doing studies for the Ford Foundation and IPOR International Research Associates. We became very good friends. When he was young, Frank had attended a seminary school in Chicago and left after an unfortunate incident of sexual harassment by a priest. This explained why, even though he was at City College and I was at Fordham, he seemed to know more about Catholicism than I ever did. We would discuss religion at times. It was Frank who first told me about Martin Luther and Calvin. When I went to Fordham and asked about Martin Luther, the Jesuits would chide me and tell me to stay away from such people because they would put my faith at risk of excommunication. Frank was my mentor, a person I looked up to because he took me out of the ghetto. He introduced me to Chinese food and life outside of Manhattan. He was there for whatever you needed, a quiet, non-judgmental person with whom you could discuss anything.

Frank was a linguist in that he spoke Portuguese, Spanish and German and taught in Brazil when he was there for the Ford Foundation. He was getting a master's degree from New York

University and a John Hay Whitney grant, gave him the opportunity to apply to Harvard for a Ph.D. When he was accepted and he suggested that I apply for a grant so that I could go to Harvard or Yale Law School. I received the scholarship and both Yale and Harvard accepted me. However, if I went to Harvard or Yale Law School, I would have to attend for an extra year because the program at Brooklyn Law School was a two-year program and did not teach common law, a requirement at both schools.

Going to Harvard would mean relocating to Massachusetts with my large family. I was worried that I had been given only a one-year scholarship but I would have to attend Harvard for two years. I did not understand at the time that once you were accepted by an Ivy League school like Harvard, you would be given whatever financial support you needed. No one ever flunked out of these schools nor left for economic reasons. I thought about it long and hard and decided to use the fellowship money to remain at Brooklyn Law School and attend full-time during the day. I even had enough money to purchase a brand new Volkswagen, which made my commute by auto instead of by subway easier. As a full-time student, I met David Dinkins, the first black mayor of New York City, who sat next to me.

When Dinkins became mayor, he would invite me to Gracie Mansion. Upon seeing me in the audience, he would remark, "There's Johnny Carro, my main man. He put me through law school".

The John Whitney Hay Fellows were treated to a luncheon at a Thai restaurant in Rockefeller Center. I had never eaten at such an exotic place and found the menu confusing. I ordered what I thought would be an exotic meal only to have it turn out to be fried rice with an egg on top; something that we Puerto Ricans eat all the time. When we did not have enough money to buy meat, so we put an egg on top of the rice and call it "huevos á caballo," which means "eggs on horseback."

I continued to work full-time as a probation officer while I went to law school during the day and my schedule was grueling. I would study on weekdays until I went to bed at 10:00 pm, get up at 2:00 am and study at the kitchen table from 2:00 to 7:00 am, when I would bathe, eat breakfast and go to work. On weekends I would go to the Aguilar Library across the street on Southern Boulevard and Tiffany Street, from 9:00 am to 5:00 pm on Saturdays and 10:00 am to 5:00 pm on Sundays at which time I prepared the week's assignments. On Friday nights Terry and I continued to go dancing at the Palladium, and on Fridays and on Saturdays, we went to the Taft, where we would take in Tito Puente, Machito, Tito Rodríguez or Vicentico Valdez. I found I could compartmentalize my life rather well. During the time I went to law school, we lived on **866** Tiffany Street with our first three children, Sherry Lyn, Chris and John. The first year was difficult because I was unfamiliar with law but I managed to make it and continue working. I also managed to find a better job working with the New York City Youth Board.

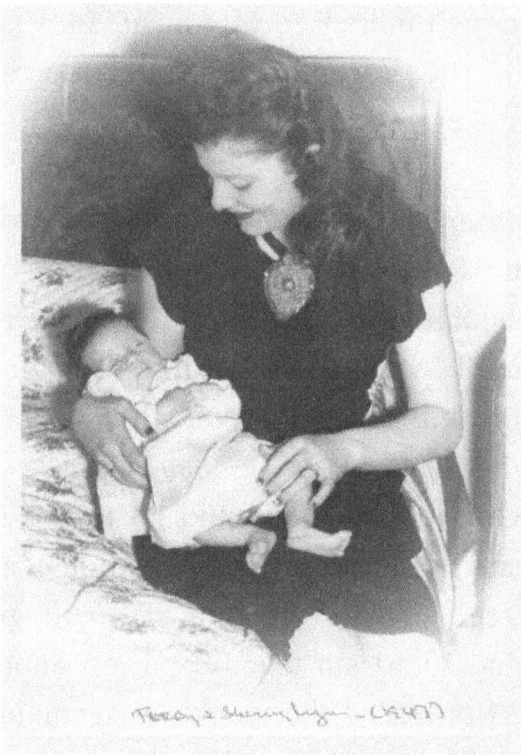

Tereza & Sherry Lyn - (1947)

In 1954, while I was still working in Children's Court, I met a police officer named Donald Fogarty, who was with the J.A.B., the Juvenile Aid Bureau and represented the Police Department in the Bronx Children's Court. We became friends and he recommended that I consider joining the Police Department and arranged for me to meet with Lieutenant Mangrum, who worked with the Juvenile Aid Bureau, under Teresa Melchione, the head of that program in the Police Department. Lt. Robert Mangrum, who was African American, told me that the Department could use a Latino worker in the South Bronx, since they had no J.A.B. person there, except for Donald Fogarty. He said that if I took the police exam and came to the Police Department, he would arrange for me to come and work in the Juvenile Aid Bureau, where I could continue going to law school.

I took Lt. Mangrum's advice and scored well on the written exam but only just barely passed the physical, where I had to run a hundred yards with a hundred pound sack. The officer in charge asked me if I wanted to raise the score on the physical by running again- I gladly declined. However, I scored well enough that I was placed on the police list. Several months later I received a call and in May of 1954, I went into the Police Department. I stayed in law school and I started as a rookie. One of the reasons I considered joining the Department was to learn about police procedures. I had decided to become a criminal defense lawyer and I was interested in what and how the police were taught about the penal law. I wanted an insider's view of how regulations were applied and followed by the police.

The Police Training Academy was on 23rd Street. We had a regular course of study in the penal law police procedure and also a series of lectures about situations that would arise. One captain who lectured us was known for a lecture he called the "three BBBs", about the things that all policemen had to be concerned about in the Department because they were fraught with dangers. The three BBBs were "Bribes, Broads and Booze." We were told not to drink from the house bottle in bars because they were reserved for greedy policemen and likely to contain something bad, like urine. We were cautioned to wear civilian clothes off duty and not to volunteer, for example, if you were on an incident on a bus, since we could wind up in all kinds of trouble. The requirements for entrance into the police department were stringent. There was a height requirement; when you took the exam, you had to be five feet eight and one half inches tall. You needed 20/20 eyesight. This seemed ridiculous to me and I could see why there were so few Puerto Ricans or Latinos in the Department since most Latinos are under five feet eight. In my case, I had to sleep on the floor for one week to make sure I was the requisite height. Nor did I understand why you needed 20/20 eyesight, since one could easily get corrective lenses. I made a mental note to consider bringing a lawsuit to change the height requirements once I became an attorney, to insure that Latino officers were not discriminated against for New York City Civil Service jobs.[10]

My experience with the Police Department was not generally a happy one. It was a segregated organization and when I first went, there was only one other Latino, Frank Uguarte, in my class and only about fifty Hispanic police officers in the entire Department. In 1954 the Police Department was overwhelmingly Irish and Italian. African Americans were in the Housing Police Department, which meant they did not have peace officer status. Everyone had their own groups, the Irish were in the Shamrock Society, the Italians were in the Columbians and the black officers were in the

---

[10] I would later be a founder of the Puerto Rican Legal Defense and Education Fund, Inc., a public interest law firm that participated in a series of landmark cases, generally know as the Guardians Association cases, the successfully challenged, among other things, height requirements that discriminated against Latinos seeking to become police officers. The Guardian cases were affirmed by the U.S. Supreme Court in 1983. 463 US 582 (1983).

Guardians. Racism was pervasive as I discovered on one of my few assignments. Officers were mostly concerned with getting "freebies," freebies at the bar, freebies at the movies, freebies here and there and scoring to make some money; all of which saddened me. I did have one or two assignments. I went to work in East Harlem in the 25th Precinct. I was in my civilian gray uniform for rookie cops and I was paired with an old timer who showed me around the neighborhood. At one point he turned to be and said, "How did they tell you to treat spics?" Before I could answer he went on, "Well let me tell you. When you see these spics hustling on a stoop, you don't go in there and say "please move." You go in and crack them on the head and tell them "MOVE!" and threaten them with your nightstick. If they say anything, just hit one over the head." I was shocked. The lectures at the Academy had not prepared me for this. For a moment I was afraid that if that cop learned my name and nationality he could use his nightstick on me.

Ironically, as it turned out, I was in great demand as a rookie. I was a Latino with experience and a college graduate, who was attending law school. Suddenly, different sections of the Police Department began attempting to get my services. There were many efforts to recruit me into one department or another, the Narcotics Division, the

Shoo Fly Squad and a number of others. Unfortunately, the demands of these jobs would not allow me to continue my law studies and I wanted to work in community programs. I finally managed to get an interview with Inspector Jones of the Juvenile Aid Bureau, a representative of Teresa Melchione. Inspector Jones reviewed my application and said that I would probably have to get some street experience before I went to the J.A.B., generally as much as five years. This would mean leaving law school. I pointed out that I had been with the Welfare Department for three years and worked in the streets for two years with Probation. His response was that lawyers at the Police Department were a dime a dozen. I asked him how many Latino lawyers did they have but he seemed puzzled by my question. At any rate, the interview did not go well. It was clear that Inspector Jones did not see me joining the J.A.B. without getting street experience in the Police Department and that meant that I would have to leave law school for a while.

I went home very disappointed that day, but I happened to read an article in the New York Times Magazine Section about working with youth gangs at the Youth Board. The article described a new program, the Street Gang Program, designed to reach out to youth gangs, not by bringing them into a center, but by going out to meet them, spending time with them to redirect their activities from anti-social to social activities. It was headed by a man named Hugh Johnson and it sounded very interesting. I called Mr. Johnson, who initially interviewed me on the phone and then asked that I come in for an interview in person. During the interview, he asked me questions about working in the field and my experiences as a minority. At the end of the interview he offered me a position with the Youth Board. The starting salary would be several hundred dollars more in salary than I was making. They would tailor my hours so I could attend law school, I would receive a small expense account and the Youth Board would allow me one week before and one week after each exam and give me six weeks to eight weeks to study for the bar examination. I was delighted, took the offer and shook hands with Mr. Johnson.

The following Monday, I reported to the Police Department, turned in my gear and announced I was resigning. I had only been there three weeks to a month and they were quite shocked but I felt I had no choice. I was going to the Youth Board because Inspector Jones had gone out of his way to discourage me from applying to the J.A.B. One of the last things he said to me during the interview was, "Listen kid, I was "on the tit" for seventeen years before I got on this job." Three days later, three representatives of the Police Department came to my house to ask if I would consider withdrawing my resignation, and promising that I could go into the Juvenile Aid Bureau. I expressed my gratitude but told them I had already made up my mind. I was looking forward to working with for the Youth Board and that was the end of that.

In the 1950's, gangs and anti-social youths began to proliferate in the City of New York resulting in gang killings and many gang related skirmishes. As a result, the Youth Board developed a program, the Street Club, or Gang Projects, that sought out the gang groups involved, and attempted to work with them in their neighborhoods. This approach was needed because these groups did not come to the youth centers and to reach them you had to go out to where they could be found. The work began in the neighborhoods of East Harlem or El Barrio, the Lower East Side and Brooklyn.

The Youth Board assigned workers to go to the neighborhoods where the gang members were and to try to induce them to engage in socially accepted behavior. Our efforts included getting them jobs, training and education; generally helping them to acquire skills. There were gangs throughout the City and they were organized into a complex web of turfs. In El Barrio, the big gangs that dominated the neighborhoods were The Dragons and the Viceroys. In the Italian neighborhood, the Red Wings controlled an area east of Lexington Avenue to Palladino Ave, generally between 110th and 118th Streets. Together, these gangs controlled the Boys' Clubs on 112th and First Avenue and the Galvani Junior High School, P.S. 83 and Benjamin Franklin High School. In the Bronx, the Italian gangs were the Golden Guineas and the Fordham Baldies in the Bellmont area. The Young Sinners were prevalent in the Latino areas of the Bronx.

The Dragons were headed by a young man named Cheyenne who attempted to expand the gang's turf up to Harlem, east and west, and the Lower East Side. Cheyenne wanted to create the Dragon Nation. L'il Abner ran the Dragons in East Harlem and his girlfriend, Gloria, was a member of the female complement of the Dragons. There was the Dragon Juniors at 103rd Street and Third Avenue, led by Little Willie. The turf of the Viceroys was 112th Street between Madison and Fifth Avenues. The leaders were the Torres brothers and several other members, among them Arecibo and Carmelo. Race was a factor that fueled gang activities. The Viceroys were black Latinos, as opposed to the Dragons who were white Puerto Ricans. However, the Viceroys did not mix with African Americans and were looked down upon by the Dragons.

I was assigned by the Youth Board to work first with the Dragons and later the Viceroys. A fellow worker, Aaron Schmais was assigned to work with the Young Lords, while Lany Borges and Vinnie Martinez worked with other groups in the area. When gang conflict erupted between two African American groups, the Bishops and El Quinto, in Brooklyn, I was transferred there to deal with the problem. I was a second year law student at Brooklyn Law School. It was the summer of 1955 and a bad time for me because I was taking Property Law, one of the most difficult courses in law school. I worked six to eight weeks, seven days a week without a break and attended law school at the same time. In Brooklyn, I met Kenny Marshall, who I recommended and who applied for the same fellowship I had- the John Hay Fellowship-, as well as Ned Llamas, who I also recommended.

My work with the gangs required that I establish relationships with gang members. If they were to trust me, I had to show confidence in them. While I was working with the Dragon Juniors in the Bronx, I decided that I had built enough of a relationship that I could bring some of them to my home. One Saturday I invited two and decided that

I would entrust them to help with babysitting while my wife and I went to the movies. It was very revealing how enthralled they were by the idea that I would invite them to my home. That was on a Saturday and everything went well. By Monday, they were telling stories about how my wife looked like Ava Gardner and describing my fantastic apartment. My home was, in fact, a two bedroom, railroad apartment above a bar on Southern Boulevard and Tiffany Street in the Bronx, but to them it could have been a palace.

It was important to the gang members that I thought enough of them to invite them to my home. As a result, I became one of the most protected workers around. Sometimes this proved to be a problem. One day, we went to the movies, the Jewel on 116th Street and went upstairs to find seats. It was very dark and I tried to sit in a seat that was already occupied. The man in the seat reacted by calling me a "mother f*cker", told me to get off him and threatened to "waste me". My protectors sprang into action, they drew guns and told me to go ahead and sit on him, because they were going to waste him. I had to calm them down quickly. I said, "Look I don't need anybody to waste anyone, it was my fault, I sat on him. Please let me handle my own situation", and fortunately they listened to me. This was how volatile the lives of these young people were. In their environment they constantly had to prove how bad and bold they were. When they were out of their element, it was another story.

I once took a group of four or five of the Dragons to the St. George Pool in Brooklyn. Once they undressed and got into bathing suits, they were defenseless. They couldn't swim well and huddled around me for protection for the entire time. When I took them hiking in New Jersey, they had a devil of a time putting up a tent. They easily gave up and came to my tent to sleep. In this situation, out of the streets, where they stared you down and carried guns, they were frightened little boys.

My work with the gangs was very fulfilling and I developed a sense of caring for the young men who became like a part of my family. In Harlem I worked with good people. Among my colleagues, Joe DiMaggio and Vinnie Riccio, a tough Marlon Brando type from Brooklyn, worked with the Italian gangs. There was Aaron Schmais, a bright, very athletic, wonderful guy, who subsequently became Dean of Men at NYU. Ned Llamas was a friend who wanted very badly to become a social worker. I finally spoke to Hugh Johnson who got him a job working with the Sinners in the Bronx. He subsequently returned to school to get a master's degree and return to the Youth Board as a supervisor.

While I was still working in Harlem, a notorious gang-related killing occurred in the Bronx. The Santana-Blankenship murder was the case of a young man from Pennsylvania who was killed by a young man from the Bronx who was Puerto Rican. That incident and another killing, the Serra murder, motivated the Youth Board to set up operations in the Bronx. I was transferred and made acting supervisor, in charge of the Youth Gang Project in the Bronx. The office was on Tremont Avenue. The Bronx also had a number of gangs, among them a division of the Young Sinners, the Dragons and Italian gangs such as the Fordham Baldies and the Golden Guineas. I assigned a worker to each gang in an effort to keep things quiet. Jerry Garfinkel worked with the Golden Guineas and Dan Murrow was assigned to the Fordham Baldies.

One Sunday, I had an encounter with a gang member that was typical of the problems we faced. Orchard Beach in the Bronx was segregated according to gang territories. I was introduced to Kenny De Vito of the Golden Guineas who very graciously thanked me for assigning to his gang, Dan Murrow a worker "who was not a spic." I pressed

Kenny about why he was so vehemently opposed to "spics" and he responded by asking, "Haven't you been with them on the subways? They smell, they stink" and he launched into ten-minute diatribe about "spics." I finally said to him, "You are very lucky that you only meet "spics" on the subway and you're not in a situation like mine where you have to live with them. I told Kenny that I was one of those "spics" he was talking about and I happened to be married to an Italian. He was more than a little nonplussed by my revelation and responded "marrone!" He was visibly embarrassed that I allowed him to go on his rant before I told him. Kenny incidentally was eventually convicted of murder and sent to prison for a long period of time. Another young man, that I met in my work in the Bronx, fared a great deal better than most of his fellow gang members. He was Dion Di Mucci, a member of the Fordham Baldies. When I met him he spent a great deal of his time smoking pot, but he went on to become Dion of Dion and the Belmonts, famous for songs like "Run Around Sue" and is now in the Rock n' Roll Hall of Fame.

One of the most memorable experiences I had while working at the Youth Board was meeting the famous playwright Arthur Miller, who wanted to write about the work of the Youth Board, possibly a play about teen gangs. He met with Vincent Riccio,

Kenny Marshall and me and hung out with us in the Bedford- Stuyvesant area for about two summer months. During these meetings he picked our brains for as much information as we could provide about youth gang work. He would take us to lunch and allow us to con him into buying us the good stuff, pastrami sandwiches with potato salad on the side and Dr. Pepper. I kidded him constantly about introducing us to Marilyn Monroe, whom he was seeing, but he was a good sport and, in fact, got a big kick from all this.

Miller wrote an outline for a play about youth gangs and he sent me a copy. I was excited when I read it because I thought it would put us on the map in terms of youth gang work. I was also looking forward to having, perhaps, Marlon Brando play the lead. The project ran into trouble because, in the City Council, Mr. Miller was considered a "pinko", a communist sympathizer and they would not authorize the play's production and the project died. This happened at a time, when Mr. Miller was about to have two plays debut on Broadway, "A View from the Bridge", and, "A Tale of Two Mondays." He sent me tickets to attend the plays, although I could not resist the opportunity to tell him that I would rather have met Marilyn Monroe.

I worked for the New York City Youth Board, from 1954 to 1958, when I resigned to go into the practice of law full-time. During my time in the Youth Board, I worked with the Council of Social and Athletic Clubs, otherwise known as the Street Club Project. It was a new program established to work with young gangs that did not go to settlement houses and were engaged in street fights and gang warfare. The idea was to reach out to them, assign workers to them to try to change their behavior from anti-social behavior to socially accepted modes. The workers would try to get them to stop fighting and to get them occupational employment, or at least to redirect them from anti-social behavior.

The program had been working in Brooklyn and Manhattan and was subsequently sent to the Bronx. It was handled by personnel who were known as street club workers, people who were experienced in working with neighborhood groups or gangs. Among them were some fairly experienced people: Vincent Riccio who worked in Brooklyn, Harrison Lightfoot, Joe DiMagio and Aaron Schmais, who worked in Manhattan; all of whom had varied backgrounds. There was no real structure for working with the clubs. You worked at a salary, depending on your education and experience and, at the time, there were no formal regulations in terms of time worked, overtime and vacations. After a while, as the program became more intensified and with more hired workers, I became to note that there was a need for structuring the programs.

There were no unions at the Youth Board at the time. I began to look into this matter and got in touch with Jerry Worth, who was the head of the Civil Service employees in the City, about the possibility of organizing this group so that they would be covered by some tenure, vacation, overtime rules and received a booklet on their benefits. Worth was amenable to this and it was decided that we would attempt to form a union of Youth Board Workers. Jerry Worth put me onto the task and I wrote a letter to James McCarthy, the head of the Youth Board, indicating that we wanted to sit down and talk about organizing the youth workers. This was not met with any sort of enthusiasm. When the letter became known, I had to go underground because they were looking to fire me for having contacted the Youth Board. I actually had to almost go undercover while negotiations proceeded. As it turned, although there was initial adverse reaction, after a time McCarthy, Johnson and the people from the Youth Board, came around to negotiating with us. We were able for the first time to establish a union of workers for the New

York City Youth Board, which provided terms and conditions as to salary, employment, overtime, vacations and tenure. Two classes of workers were created: senior workers and regular street care workers. A contract was signed to this effect. It was a momentous occasion, the first time we had a union at the New York City Youth Board. I was very happy as it was my first attempt at union organizing and I was gratified by the results.

Chapter Eight
Community, Politics and the Practice of Law

I was not active in the community or politics until I finished law school and was admitted to the bar in 1956. I began to practice law while still working for the Youth Board. My friend, Salvador "Jesse" Almeida, a real estate broker rented me space in his office at 850 Longwood Avenue in the Bronx and I was able to hang up my shingle. I managed to structure my schedule so that I worked at the Youth Board from 4:00 pm to 11:00 pm and then spent mornings and days attempting to learn my craft as a lawyer. I did whatever legal matters came up. I bought "Horowitz' Lawyer's Manual," which explained how to set up a new law practice. I handled the sale of businesses, the chartering of clubs, small family and criminal court matters, getting the licenses for beer applications and other aspects of a general practice. At the same time, I became involved with community groups who needed charters or wanted to incorporate, work that I would do routinely in subsequent years. I would help the organization create a group who would apply for the charter. I would write by-laws, a constitution and register the organization with the state. I charged very little for this work, gave them my business card and I became known by various groups.

I stayed with the Youth Board until 1958, after which I resigned to develop my law practice full-time. It had become increasing difficult to go to court during the day and then work evenings and weekends. I had a family that included several children. I found it increasingly difficult to juggle family life with my law practice while working at the Youth Board.

While working in my new office at 946 Prospect Avenue, I met a young African American attorney, Frazier Davidson, who was interested in sharing a practice. I severed my relationship with Almeida when he told me he wanted a piece of my action as a lawyer. I told him that we could not do that because he was not an attorney and that I could only pay him for office space. This lead to an amicable parting of the ways and I set up a two-room office to practice law with Frazier at 946 Prospect Avenue. We were not partners, but associates who shared the work and covered the office. The practice was located at 163rd and Prospect Avenue, only a block away from my home. I spent several thousand dollars in furnishing it. I was quite happy to begin devoting myself to the full-time practice of law.

Community, Politics and the Practice of Law   Chapter Eight / 111

When I began practicing law full-time, I met a Manhattan attorney named Seymour Ostrow at the Bronx Supreme Court. I watched him try a murder case and I could see that he was an excellent attorney. Sy practiced in East Harlem with Mark Lane, who later became a member of the State Assembly. We got to know each other and began to discuss our future over dinner. Sy graduated from Yale Law School. He was interested in the Puerto Rican and Latino community, specifically the specialty of criminal law. He was well known in East Harlem for his work with the Puerto Rican community. We found that we had much in common particularly with respect to serving the community and our interest in the local practice of law. After several discussions, we decided to become partners. We sealed the deal with a handshake and located offices downtown at 150 Broadway, where I remained until 1966.

I did not make my way into politics the routine way by joining a local club, sweeping floors and waiting to be considered for an appointment. I bypassed all that when I was asked to run a Citizens' Committee for candidates at the top of the ticket. In 1964, I decided to run for Congress in the 22nd C.D., I did so of my own volition. I had analyzed the data and determined that the Bronx 22nd Congressional District had become principally a minority community. The incumbent white group and their representative, who had been there for five terms and his white constituents, had, by and large, moved out of the community. I decided to run against the incumbent Democrat, Jack Gilbert, who had been there several terms. The regular organization saw this as a threat and did everything possible to prevent me from winning. They went so far as to run an African American and two Latino candidates against me in the primary, thereby assuring the incumbent Gilbert's win.

Despite my loss, I had gained the experience of running my own campaign. I had recruited supporters, opened two campaign offices and managed to poll nearly 6,000 votes in the primary, as opposed to my opponent's 11,000 votes. As a result, I believe that I paved the way for Herman Badillo who entered the race in the same district in 1967. Unlike me, Herman ran with Paul Screvane's mayoral ticket and won. He was swept into office by a landslide victory for the Democrats. Politically at the time, we had very little. A few Puerto Ricans belonged to some of the regular Democratic clubs and in order to get anywhere there you had to go in and be in for several years. Only in one area, East Harlem, we had one third of a political district where the leader was Antonio "Tony" Mendez. He was located at 102nd Street and Fifth Avenue. It was from there that our first politicians emanated, among them were Manuel Gomez, Herman Badillo, José Ramos Lopez and Emilio Nuñez. Manny Gomez had been named Deputy Commissioner of Aviation and I believe Emilio Nuñez was a judge in Special Sessions Court. Ramos Lopez subsequently became an Assemblyman from the Bronx.

In 1960 Robert Wagner decided to run for a third term as Mayor of New York City. This was unprecedented because he was opposed by the regular organizations that baulked at supporting him. Hortense Gabel, my political "madrina" godmother, told the Mayor about me and suggested that I organize a group to meet with Wagner, with a view towards working on his campaign. I put together a group of ten people, among them Herman Badillo, Frank Torres, Max Gonzalez, Julio Sabater and me. A meeting was set up at Gracie Mansion. I remembered the words of Ray Jones, Congressman Powell's Campaign Manager, about there being a "quid pro quo" in politics, and I created an agenda of items to discuss with Wagner in case he asked us to work for him. I was the spokesperson for the group and Mayor Wagner indeed asked for our help with his campaign. I pointed out to him that he had been Mayor for two terms, eight years and that I could count on one hand the number of Puerto Ricans that he had named to office. If he wanted us to work for him that would have to change. Our *quid pro quo* for working for him was that we wanted to get one judicial position, a judgeship, one Assistant to the Mayor, two Deputy Commissioners and several other lesser jobs. Mayor Wagner said he would look into this and get back to us. Several days after the meeting, I got a call telling me that the Mayor agreed to our conditions and asked us to give him names. We recommended Felipe Torres for a future judgeship, Herman Badillo for Assistant to the Mayor, Max Gonzalez for Deputy Commissioner and several others. I did not submit my name for a job at the time. Several days later, the Mayor's Office contacted me and informed me that they did not think that Herman Badillo should get the job as Assistant to the Mayor since he was a political figure. Herman had just lost a leadership race to Congressman Freddie Santangelo in East Harlem and the Mayor's people thought that it would be better to name a person who was not that politically involved. Since I was the President of the Puerto Rican Bar Association, which was not political, they had decided to offer me the position. This did not meet with joy from Herman, but the Mayor instead decided to offer him the position Commissioner of Relocation in the City of New York. Housing and Relocation was a very big thing at the time. Wagner agreed that he would give us a couple of deputies.

This decision resulted in Max Gonzalez becoming a Deputy Commissioner of Markets and Ortíz of the Ortíz Funeral Homes became Deputy Fire Commissioner, although that was not our "placement." He was someone who had made a big contribution to Deputy Mayor Cavanaugh for the Mayor. Louie Hernández, a political leader from Brooklyn, was also to be named to a position, and the Mayor said he would still hold off until he was elected to give us the judgeship. We agreed.

Although I was told at Gracie Manson that I was becoming Assistant to the Mayor I was disheartened to receive paperwork that identified me as Assistant for Press Relations. I made it clear that that was not the job we had requested and I would not accept it. We wanted the job of Assistant to the Mayor, a position formerly held by Bob Lowe, who was going to the City Council. We wanted the same duties, the same salary and all the things that went with the position of Assistant to the Mayor. I told them that once the matter was straightened out I would come to work for the Mayor as agreed. Several days later, I received a call and was told that the matter had been corrected. A press release was issued that named me Assistant to the Mayor. As Assistant to the Mayor, I would be located in City Hall and placed in charge of the Mayor's Information Center. I would also be the Mayor's representative to social agencies and I would be in charge of dealing with the Latino community. I would help handle the Mayor's schedule of meetings with the Latino community. If there were events in the Latino community he couldn't attend I would appear on his behalf. I agreed to this and Miss Ann Paris was assigned to be my secretary. My offices would be in City Hall directly below the Mayor's office. This was the first time a Puerto Rican was named Assistant to the Mayor, an occasion that was very warmly greeted by El Diario newspaper and the Latino community.

My Swearing-In as Assistant to the Mayor

I was one of four Assistants to the Mayor with a net salary of $18,500[11]. The other Assistants were Bernard Rugieri, Jim Wilson and Harold Weisman. The responsibility of Mayoral agencies was divided among the four of us. In addition to running the Mayor's Information Center and handling the overflow of appointments, I was the liaison to several social agencies including the Youth Board and the Department of Welfare. I made it my mission to make the presence of Puerto Ricans in the City known to the Mayor. I kept the Mayor's Office so busy that his secretary, Mrs. Kelly, complained that that she couldn't even spell the names of all the Latinos that had appointments with the Mayor. My response to her complaints was "get used to it, that's my job, to open doors for our community with the Mayor."

One of the duties I undertook was to get various agencies, such as the Police Department and Sanitation and Housing, to give the Mayor's Office a list of the Latino people working for them. This was necessary since we didn't know how many Latinos were employed by the City. Many agencies had ethnic organizations to represent the employees. The Police Department had the Shamrock Society

---

[11] In the present day, "Assistant to the Mayor" is known as "Deputy Mayor."

for the Irish, the Columbians for the Italians; the Fire Department had the Vulcans for black employees. There were no Hispanic organizations within the various departments and we wanted to foster the establishment of Hispanic societies in Police, Sanitation, Housing and other City agencies. This was not possible without a list of names of Hispanic employees. There were problems at first. Initially I had difficulty getting names from Anna Cross, the Commissioner of Corrections. This surprised me because she was a good friend of the Puerto Rican Mayor of San Juan, Felicia Rincón de Gautier who often came to New York for the Puerto Rican Parade. She would meet with Anna Cross, who would take her to Riker's Island to visit. I had to invoke the Mayor's name before I got about forty or fifty names. We met with some of these people to determine if they were interested getting a charter and getting organized and become officially recognized in the Department. I proceeded to do this for the Police, for Housing, Sanitation and eventually organized Hispanic societies in Civil Service. This was a wonderful accomplishment. At some point, I learned that Spanish and Puerto Rican Grocers' Association, which represented over 15,000 groceries in the City, were not organized. Helping them to organize gave me the opportunity to get to know them and understand their needs as small businesses. During the course of my work I began attending the meetings of the City Council. I came to appreciate that politics is the science of government.

When I worked at Welfare as a provisional, I could never get more than nine months credit for Civil Service, so I could never qualify to take the test to become a social worker, which required one year. At the Youth Board, I was also provisional and seldom, if ever, met with those who ran the agency such as Ralph Whelan or James McCarthy. As Assistant to the Mayor, I was the liaison person between the Mayor's Office and the Youth Board and a number of other agencies. It was my job to set up meetings between the Commissioner of the Youth Board and the Mayor. So suddenly, a person who couldn't qualify to become a supervisor at the Youth Board, I was now consulted in order to set up a meeting between the Commissioner and the Mayor.

The experience of working for the Mayor, allowed me to meet Latino groups throughout the City and continue to hone my skills in public speaking. I did not have an active law practice. I believe I was a born social worker and I enjoyed working with people and getting involved in the problems of people from all walks of life. The Mayor made me his liaison to the Puerto Rican

Parade and when dignitaries came for the annual parade, it was my job to schedule them to come to City Hall and to work with their itinerary. I made it a point to meet many of the mayors from Puerto Rico and one evening I invited them to my home. I met famous Puerto Ricans as Pagán de Colón, Fernándo Sierra Berdecia, Leo Cabranes and the leaders and mayors of all Puerto Rican hometowns.

Interviewing Gov. of PR Luiz Muñoz Marin.

Many years earlier, when I was in the ROTC at Fordham, I marched in the Puerto Rican Parade. Now I was on the reviewing stand with the Mayor and other dignitaries. Around 1958, was the beginning of the Puerto Rican Parade, which came to rival the St. Patrick's Day Parade. We had the advantage of better weather since our Parade was the second week in June, while the St. Patrick's Day Parade was in March, when it was still cold.

I worked at City Hall as Assistant to the Mayor from 1960 to 1965, when the Mayor's term expired. He had served three terms and Mayor John Lindsay was making a bid to become the first Republican Mayor of New York. When you are a political appointee, you serve at the behest of the elected official. The day I was hired by the Mayor I signed a letter of resignation that he could accept at any time. We knew that our work would end when the Mayor left office. Lindsay was young, good-looking and articulate. He had a good chance of defeating Wagner so there were already several people vying for my job.

When Lindsay won, I was invited to come down to Puerto Rico, bring a "New York Green Book", where I spent three days identifying the positions in the various City departments and offices, to which they should seek appointments from the new Mayor. I was asked if I was interested in becoming Deputy Commissioner of Markets and other similar positions. I declined, saying that when I left office, it was my intention to go back to the private practice of law. I entertained the idea of going to Washington for a while and getting a job with the Democrats in Washington but decided not to do so because relocating the whole family was not something that I looked forward to. Besides, I liked New York and wanted to stay.

My job ended on December 31, 1965 and shortly after Lindsay took office in January of 1966, most of the City's unions decided to go on strike during the first two weeks of January. Although Mayor Wagner appointed the father of Frank Torres, Felipe N. Torres, to a judgeship in Family Court, as promised, however, Lindsay, unlike Wagner, did not appoint any Puerto Rican or Latino Deputy Commissioners. It wasn't until he decided to run for another term in 1969, that it behooved Lindsay, to appoint more Latinos to office. I turned down the offer, a position as Deputy Commissioner of Markets, by the Lindsay people and prepared to open a practice. The City was closed for two weeks because of the strike in January 1966, so my plans were delayed, leaving me with no source of income for that period. I returned to practice in the Bronx. Sy Ostrow and I terminated our practice at 160 Broadway. Our lease was up and he had looked at premises in the Woolworth Building, at 233 Broadway; a whole floor which rented for about $14,000 a year. Our practice had not done very well because I was away often at City Hall. The work was not coming in and I had to subsidize the office by donating part of my salary which generally amounted to $100 monthly. Sy wanted to rent offices to other lawyers, but I was not interested in becoming a landlord and I worried about a fourteen-year lease.

We parted ways amicably and I decided to go back to my roots in the Bronx where I felt that I would have a better shot of developing as a lawyer and starting a new practice after an absence of four years, I was able to find a small office about one block from the Bronx Criminal Court, at 407 East 161st Street, which consisted of two rooms. There was a front room for interviews, where people came in and a rear office for me and a bathroom. I did not have a secretary, but I was able to use one of the women who worked for me at City Hall, Julie Soto, and a young lady whom I had met, Toni Henson, who was an excellent secretary. Toni came in and worked part time, on weekends or whenever I needed her. I would constantly have work prepared for her. She worked consistently and managed to organize the office in a very agreeable way. She was wonderful and I am very thankful to her.

When I first started, after having been away from my Bronx practice while I was at City Hall, it was difficult. I devoted time to going to the Bronx Criminal Court to just sit and reacquaint myself with the law and learned what had changed since I left practice several years before. I introduced myself to some of the assistants in the Part, told them I was not there to solicit cases but to observe the proceedings. Among the people I met were, Stanley Parness and Al Nierenberg. Parness subsequently became a judge. The people I met were nice and taught me a great deal. In those days the Bronx had very few Latino lawyers and a handful of African Americans lawyers, but many available clients. The Legal Aid Society handled only the more serious cases. People appeared in court who could not afford a lawyer, and in response, judges sitting on the bench would just call and ask you to do the Court a favor. You would give the client your card and assume the case for the court appearance. If a fee materialized it was good, but otherwise the case would be pro bono. There was enough volume that I found myself handling fifteen to thirty cases a week. When you took all these cases and multiplied whatever you got, twenty-five, fifty dollars per case with approximately fifteen cases, you start to do fairly well in a short time.

The first year I worked by myself, I earned $36,000. During the second year I earned $70,000. In the third year, 1969, I had negligence case, which I referred out to some successful personal injury lawyers. It involved a woman, Mrs. Bordon, who was apparently a victim of negligence. There had been medical malpractice and the lawyers handling it for me were able to settle it for several hundred thousand dollars. I received a check for $40,000, an amount that about exceeded what I made in a year of practice. I was almost tempted to begin a civil practice, but I was more interested in criminal work and being a defense lawyer.

During the time that I began to practice law again, New York State held a Constitutional Convention. I received a call from the leader of the Pontiac Regular Democratic Club, Eugene Rodríguez, who asked me if I would be one of the three delegates from his club to run for representative from the 22nd Congressional District. Eugene Rodríguez was a successful lawyer who was the first Puerto Rican to be elected State Senator from the Bronx. He had been the leader of the Pontiac Regular Democratic Club, but was subsequently indicted for tampering with a witness in a matter he was handling. He was tried and convicted and went to jail and was never heard from again. Mr. Rodríguez was eventually replaced by

Robert García as State Senator, who went on to be elected to the U.S. Congress.

Eugene Rodríguez knew that I had been President of the Puerto Rican Bar Association and Assistant to the Mayor. I would be running with the regular Democratic organization for the New York State Constitutional Convention with Leo Levy, who was the Clerk of Bronx County Supreme Court and one other candidate. It meant that I would run against Herman Badillo and two of his friends who were on the reform slate. I thought about it, and given that I would be paid $17,000 for maybe one or two days weekly in Albany, I decided to do it. Herman was not too thrilled when he found out I would be running on the opposing slate, competing for the same slots. He was part of a reform group running against the organization and only three people could be elected from the 22nd District. We campaigned and defeated two of the three reform candidates, although Herman himself won, because he was also endorsed by the Liberal Party, while his running partners were not. Antónia Pantoja, Joaquín Rivera, and a young man whom I knew at Brooklyn Law School, and who was blind, Gilbert Ramirez, were also chosen as Convention delegates.

As a delegate to the Constitutional Convention of the State of New York for the 22nd

Congressional District, I would go to Albany during the year to try to enact a new constitution for New York State. At that convention I made many friends, among them David Dinkins, my classmate at Brooklyn Law School who would subsequently became Mayor, and Andy Tyler, my Yonkers neighbor who was a Supreme Court Justice and Richard Brown who subsequently would become D.A. of Queens County and was a close ally of Governor Hugh Carey. The convention was headed by Anthony Travia, a former federal judge and one of the many judges in attendance. I learned a great deal although we did not succeed in getting a new constitution for New York. The effort to rewrite the Constitution was defeated due to issues surrounding the Blaine Amendment, which bars the use of public funds to support religious education. It was an amazing experience for me in terms of the politics of New York City and the people who were fellow delegates.

In 1968, I became the Director of the Democratic Citizens' Committee for the Election of Robert F. Kennedy in the Latino community during his run for President. There was a time that I became so disillusioned with politics that I left it altogether, particularly after the assassination of Robert F. Kennedy on June 5, 1968. The New York primary for this was scheduled for June 8, 1968 and things looked great since Bobby had won the Primary in California on June 5th with a resounding victory. I believed that he was well on the way to winning the New York Primary in '68 and becoming the candidate for President. This is when tragedy struck and Robert Kennedy was assassinated in L.A. That was a bitter blow for our country and especially hard for me, since I had previously been the Chairman of the Jack Kennedy Election Committee when he ran for election in 1960. The greatest irony was that eleven years earlier, I had been the probation officer for a young Harvey Lee Oswald; he was eleven years old, when he and his mother lived in New York.

In 1968, the Democratic Convention was held in Chicago. Hubert Humphrey and Gene McCarthy were in the running with Bobby Kennedy, vying for the presidential nomination. This was also the year that the Chicago Police brutalized Flower Children at demonstrations and neither Humphrey nor McCarthy, spoke out or tried to do a thing about it. I was so appalled by what I saw, that I decided to quit politics. No more running for office and campaigns for me. I was so demoralized, that for the first time, I did not vote in a presidential election and Richard Nixon won. I regretted that and vowed never to fail to vote again.

I quit politics and directed myself to developing a law practice. I had left Wagner in '66, when Lindsay became Mayor. He was a Republican. I dissolved my practice with Seymour Ostrow and rented a small office in the Bronx and decided to go it alone in a solo practice. It wasn't long before things changed. I was offered a job with the State Commission Against Discrimination, an agency of then Governor, Averell Harriman. I took the position and was named a Field Representative. I put my practice on the shelf for the time being, since that was a full-time job. The State Commission Against Discrimination was headed by Elmer Carter, a Republican. Carter's mission was to investigate discrimination in employment, race, age and sexual orientation.

Soon after I started working, I was given a leave of absence to work in the campaign to re-elect Harriman as Governor and Frank Hogan to the Senate. This was arranged by my old friend, Hortense Gabel, who was actively working on the campaign. I knew Hortie from the time we worked on the Kennedy campaign. She was then on the staff of Robert Weaver who was Director of Housing, the Housing Commissioner under Governor Harriman. The campaign was headquartered at the Hotel Biltmore. I worked evenings and weekends. During my time at the headquarters, I recruited Frank Bonilla and Max Gónzalez to join Citizens for Harriman and Hogan. We were to develop campaign literature and organize neighborhood groups in Manhattan, Bronx and Brooklyn. Citizens for Harriman and Hogan began with a budget of $3000 which grew to $50,000. I hired a bilingual secretary, Dorothy Senerchia, to run the volunteer office, which attracted a lot of people who wanted to work distributing literature and buttons.

We established neighborhood groups in the Bronx, Manhattan, Lower East Side and Brooklyn. Congressman Adam Clayton Powell was also involved in the Harriman-Hogan campaign, as was his campaign manager, Ray Jones, known as the "Gray Fox," whom I got to know quite well. I also met Congressman Powell's future wife, Yvette Flores, who was Puerto Rican. We came up with a slogan, "Abe Sabe," meaning "Abe Knows" and had an initial rendering of 10,000 buttons with the slogan that became quite popular. It also became something of a joke. When people asked, "what is Abe Sabe?" I would say he doesn't know a damn thing, but they don't know that he doesn't know it. It was my job to schedule appearances for the candidate in Manhattan.

I became friendly with two Hogan aides, Carl Rubino and Richard Long, who had also taken leaves from Manhattan D.A. Hogan's Office, to work in his campaign for Senator. They suggested that I should join the New York County D.A.'s Office when I finished working on the campaign because they had no Puerto Rican attorneys. Julius C.C. Edelstein was the Director of the campaign and he would eventually become Deputy Mayor for Bob Wagner. My law practice was growing and I relied on Frasier Davidson, to help me out since I was involved in the campaign. I also became good friends with Ray Jones. He told me two things to remember if I ever considered going into politics. The first was, to "keep your friends close and your enemies closer." The second was "in politics you take care of your friends," and that there is a "quid pro quo" in this business. In other words, if I do for you, what will you do for me?

I worked long and hard on the Harriman campaign. One of the reasons I was asked to work on the campaign was because Rockefeller, the Republican candidate for Governor, was active in the Latino community. He had various interests in Puerto Rico and in South American and he spoke Spanish. We had to make efforts to get out the Latino vote on behalf of Harriman and the Latino community.

I got to know Governor Harriman, well enough to take him to several meetings in the Latino community. It always astounded me, that despite being an Ambassador for The U.N., he really was very austere and not a very good campaigner. He never seemed to know what was happening. On election night, when Harriman lost to Rockefeller by 11,000 votes, I went to campaign headquarters at the Waldorf Astoria. I remember the occasion clearly because he greeted me as if for the first time. I was surprised and said, "You know my name." He then thanked me for the efforts we had made on his behalf.

During the campaign, I met George Backer, who was one of Harriman's top people. Mr. Backer had his own law firm on Wall Street and his brother was Fred Backer, a Family Court judge. Mr. Backer was also the husband of Dorothy Schiff, the owner of the New York Post. His daughter, Sally Kramarsky, was also involved in the Harriman campaign and we became good friends. Before the election wound up, Mr. Backer called me to his office where he handed me a check for $10,000 to keep the Citizen's Campaign for Harriman-Hogan going. I tried, but as it happens in politics, after a couple of weeks the interest in the Harriman campaign waned. I did not think I could endure the effort going so I called Mr. Backer. I went back to his office and returned the check for the $10,000. This was a big surprise, I don't think this was done in politics and I made a lasting impression on Mr. Backer. He asked if I was interested in working on Wall Street in a job which did not involve politics. He said that he would hire me, and that in a few years time, I would earn a substantial amount of money, a six figure salary, if I decided to work for them. I was tempted and gave it some thought, but after a few days decided that I wanted to stay in public service. I thanked him for his interest and his offer.

One incident that I have a recollection of vividly was working in the Harriman-Hogan campaign. Two of Mr. Hogan's people, Richard Long and Carl Rubino had recommended that I apply to the Manhattan D.A.'s Office for a job. It appears that they had no Latinos. They had one fellow, Manuel Guerrero, who was a Spaniard related to Judge Nuñez, who was an A.D.A, but he had changed his legal name to Manuel Gregory and it was not known that he was Latino. I doubt that he even spoke Spanish. At any rate, I took Richard Long's advice when I left the Harriman campaign and I applied for a position in the Manhattan D.A.'s Office, knowing that they had no Latinos working there. I passed the first of several interviews successfully and was on the fourth interview when I encountered some difficulty. It appears that I arrived ten minutes late to meet with Richard Kuh. I apologized, telling him about the parking and the traffic situation. When he raised the question of my lateness for the third time in my interview, I inquired whether I had to genuflect, that I had apologized already, and inquired whether we were going to delve into discussing merits during the interview. I believe he was unhappy with my retort and the interview went south thereafter. For one, he noted that I had gone to Brooklyn Law School and later told me that most of the people in Mr. Hogan's office had gone to Columbia. I did not stay silent at that remark. I mentioned that my mother told me that what counts in life is not where you attended school, but what is in your head and your heart. He didn't appear too happy with that remark. He mentioned that he hoped I didn't consider going into the office because I was a Puerto Rican. I remarked that while I was a Puerto Rican I also had a law degree, just like all of the other people in the office. It was my view that good government was representative government and I felt that the office in Manhattan, which totaled over four hundred Assistant D.A.'s, could use a Latino in their office. The community consisted of one million Puerto Ricans, therefore having a Latino representative was necessary for good governance.

Incidentally, the interviewer, Richard Kuh, had been the D.A. in charge of Special Sessions Court. He was supposed to be a very hard-nosed person. Needless to say upon my telling him this I didn't survive the interview and was turned down for the A.D.A. position. Years later, after Mr. Kuh had left the D.A.'s Office, and I had become a criminal court judge in the Bronx, he happened to appear before me. I asked him to approach the bench and quietly informed him that I owed my job as a criminal court judge to him. He smiled and seemed happy at the thought. Then I informed him that his rejection of me for the D.A.'s job is what had later resulted in my being where I was now as a judge. I thanked him and asked what I could do for him and how I could help. It was one of the most happy and satisfying moments of my life.

During this period, I was also beginning to get involved in the community in the Bronx. A local Democratic club, the Wagner Democratic Club had opened. It was a reform organization and not part of the regular political organization. It was headed by the Torres family, Felipe Torres and Frank Torres, and I joined the club for a while. I met Antónia, or Toni Pantoja, a community worker whose job with the city was to bring Puerto Ricans together and work with us. Out of this evolved a group, the Puerto Rican Leadership Forum, which included, Frank Torres, Max Gónzalez, Herman Badillo, Frank Bonilla, Gene Calderón and several others who began to discuss involvement in our community. The Puerto Rican community now numbered over a million in the City of New York, and like other sectors of the population, the people had tremendous needs. They had legal needs, which included criminal and civil areas such as housing and welfare problems as well as many health and education concerns. The only agency that existed at the time for servicing these needs was the Commonwealth of Puerto Rico's, Department of Labor and Migration, which was located on West 45th Street. The Commonwealth Office was headed by Joe Monserat, who was involved in so many things that he was, for all intents and purposes, Mr. Puerto Rican. Unfortunately, Mr. Monserat never worked to increase the leadership in our community, by tapping into groups consisting of recent graduates of law school and those beginning professional careers. He had a virtual monopoly on any information that was important to our community but never shared any of it with those of us who wanted to be of service, nor recommended us for work in the overall American community.

In 1958, a study was released that showed that Puerto Ricans were at the bottom of the education system. Less than one per cent of those graduating from high school were taking Regents courses and going on to college. Without the ability to pass entrance examinations required for many jobs or some college training, Puerto Ricans were condemned to low wage jobs and disproportionate rates of unemployment. It seemed that there were more Puerto Ricans in the prison system than there were in the educational system. There was also a dire need for professionals. There were fewer than fifty Latino attorneys in the entire City and very few in other vital professions such as social work, health, education and medicine. Our people had great difficulty getting assistance with their housing and social services problems.

In response to this situation we organized the Puerto Rican-Hispanic Leadership Forum. The group included, Paco Trilla, Max Gónzalez, Frank Bonilla, Fréderico Aquino Bermudez, Gene Calderón, Blanca Cedeño, Marta Valle and me. We started meeting once a week at Max Gónzalez' office on 23rd Street. We obtained a state charter with the help of Hortense Gabel, who was then with Weiss Rifkind Wharton & Harrison law firm, helped with meeting the requirements for getting not-for-profit tax status, which she helped us secure.

There was also the newly created Puerto Rican Bar Association. I joined when it was only a year old and numbered about thirty lawyers. Unfortunately, the organization was not especially interested in giving back to their community. During my term as President in 1960, I made the mistake of proposing that each of the thirty some odd attorneys devote one day a week to a rent clinic in Manhattan. For this I was berated and called a communist. The lawyers made it clear that they were not there to do pro bono work but to try to make some money and establish their practices.

Before this new organization began to form, most of the efforts to help Latino community were provided by home town groups from Puerto Rico. Groups such as, Orocoveños Aúsentes, Caborojeños would get themselves a little clubhouse or rent one, and use it to provide birthdays, weddings and small affairs for this group. The one big event that began at about this time, the Annual Puerto Rican Day Parade, received a lot of fanfare and had many people working on it. Other than devoting their time to this and joining fledging political clubs, many of our leaders did little in the way of dealing with the problems of our people.

The dismal performance of our young people in school mobilized us to apply for grants from some of the foundations to tackle this problem. We applied to the Mellon Foundation, then headed by Steven Currier. We met for lunch with Mr. Currier, and his very large dog, at his offices on the top floor of 666 Fifth Avenue. Toni Pantoja, Frank Bonilla and I attended and made our presentation. While we spoke, Mr. Currier seemed to be doodling on a piece of paper. I thought he was paying no attention to us. As he was doodling, Mr. Currier suddenly tore out a piece of paper and handed it to me. It was a check for $100,000. I was flabbergasted; I had never seen a check for $100,000, which equated to five million today. This was the first grant we ever received and we used it for meaningful services for the community. We invested the money in the Puerto Rican Hispanic Leadership Forum and Aspira, which were one organization at the time. We felt that because of the nature of the educational needs of our people, we decided to split off Aspira, which means "aspire" from the Puerto Rican Forum and make it an entity solely devoted to having children remain in school. We chartered Aspira and hired Toni Pantoja, who left the City job of social worker, to be the first Executive Director of Aspira. We also created in a board of Directors that included Frank Bonilla as President, me as Vice President, Blanca Cedeño, Paco Trilla, Max Gonzalez, Luís Olmos and several other people as members. We searched for an appropriate location and finally settled on a place on 72nd Street, between Broadway and Amsterdam. From the first offices of Aspira, we began to create programs and make our name known to the Latino community. Today there are Aspira clubs in high schools and nationally. Its budget is $32 million, a far cry from the $100,000 we started with in 1961.

As time went on, I became involved in many more civic activities. I was asked along with Frank Bonilla to speak at a conference at Columbia University on Latinos in New York. My speech was about the plight of Puerto Ricans in New York City, in general, and what if anything was being done to improve conditions. I pointed out that, the City had no more than a handful of Puerto Ricans in meaningful jobs and that we needed people to serve in government or public administration. Frank Bonilla gave the keynote address, which was wonderful. The theme was that we did not require preferential treatment, just access to opportunity. In Spanish the theme was, "*El Puertoriqueño no pide que le den, sino que lo donde hay,*" Puerto Ricans don't ask for a handout, but rather, to be allowed to put them where there is, meaning, to let us get our foot in the door and we'll do the rest. Meanwhile, now that we had spun off Aspira to concentrate on education, we needed a new agenda for the Puerto Rican Leadership Forum and continued our effort to develop leadership in the community and open doors in the various agencies and boards in the City.

I knew that private practice would be a struggle. When I left City Hall, I was out of work for two weeks due to a City strike at that time when I had four children, three cars and a house in Yonkers. I was not at all sure that my practice would succeed. On a trip to Washington to be admitted to the Supreme Court of the United States, the group that I travelled with shared the bus with Frank Torres, who felt compelled to tell me how difficult private practice was. He was so negative that I went home feeling completely depressed. In the end, I managed to develop and have a successful small neighborhood practice in the Bronx that had few expenses. In 1968, I learned that Mary Johnston Lowe, who was the head of the NAACP and an African American lawyer practicing in the Bronx, left her partnership and was now in a solo practice. I knew Ms. Lowe before she was with the NAACP and admired and respected her. I was earning $130,000 to $140,000 a year and I had too many cases, way more than I could handle. I needed help and I couldn't think of a finer person to work with than Mary Johnston Lowe, who was a first rate lawyer.

She attended Brooklyn Law School and we knew each other casually. We met and talked and discovered we liked each other and had the same concerns and agreed to become partners. So in 1969, we began the firm of Carro and Lowe working out of my office at 407 East 161st Street in the Bronx. In the summer of the same year, I got a call from Michael Dontzin, the liaison to Mayor Lindsay, who asked me if I was interested in a judgeship. I said I had no interest in Civil Court or Family Court, but perhaps might be amenable to a Criminal Court judgeship. There was only one problem; it paid $30,000, so I left the door open at the time. However, when the Mayor called to make me the offer, I told him that I would decline and he was somewhat surprised.

I declined not only because the judgeship only paid $30,000 but also because the appointment was not even a full ten-year term, I would just serve the 2 ½ year balance of the term of a judge who had vacated the position. Given my family obligations I didn't think I could afford it and did not want to risk the insecurity of serving a partial term. Most importantly, I had just become partners with Mary Johnston Lowe, and with the size of the African American and Latino population in the Bronx and Manhattan, I believed a Puerto Rican and an African American lawyer would do very well in a joint practice. Ms. Lowe was an experienced attorney who had tried many homicide cases and we had agreed that I would handle Manhattan and she would handle the Bronx.

I declined the offer without giving the Mayor any reasons and he asked me to think it over. This was on a Friday or Saturday and he gave me until Tuesday to consider the offer. I was not prepared for what happened after that. He must have told people that he offered me a judgeship and I had turned it down because that weekend I began getting calls from Tony Mendez and other political leaders, telling me that I was crazy not to take the job. There were only two Puerto Ricans in the City with judgeships, José Ramos Lopez in the Civil Court and Manny Gomez in Criminal Court and yet we numbered over a million people in the City. I was told in no uncertain terms that I owed it to the community. My initial response was that I didn't owe the community anything but that I did owe my family. It would be a tremendous sacrifice to leave a situation where I made over $100,000 for $30,000. At the time, several other people were applying for a judgeship, among them Manuel Ramos, the former Bronx Assistant DA, who had been my classmate at Brooklyn Law School, who was now in private practice, as well as Antonio Figueroa, who had worked with me at Welfare and who had married

Joe Monserrat's secretary, Annie Figueroa. Monserrat was the head of the Puerto Rico Department of Labor and Immigration, and he was pushing for his appointment. I decided to accept and become a criminal court judge.

I had never looked forward to being a judge. I looked at it with some trepidation. It bothered me that I was leaving a practice where I was looking forward to working with Mary Johnston Lowe and that I was not particularly enthused about being a judge. I liked being on my own, taking cases of my choice as opposed to being confined to a specific space in a particular court. However, despite all of these trepidations, I decided to take the judgeship and accept it. Now the problem was to look for someone to replace me in the office. The President of the Puerto Rican Bar Association, Austin Lopez, called me and wanted to take my place. This presented a problem because Mary Johnston Lowe had just tried a case with him and wasn't too keen on working with him. He also made the mistake of saying to me, "Don't worry John. If you don't get your reappointment after 2 ½ years, I'll consider taking you back." I think that may have decided things. Mary and I settled on George Levine, an attorney who had worked for Henry Rothblat, a well-known Bronx attorney and partner of Joe Suarez. I mentioned him to Mary, who liked him and after meeting with George, he liked the idea and we decided that he would be my replacement. George was an experienced, confident, wonderful human being whom I would get to know and grew to love more and more the more I got to know him.

When the Mayor called that Tuesday and urged me to accept the offer, I did. In the meantime, when Mr. Ramos learned I was being named a judge, it ended our friendship. I incurred his enmity and we were never close again. I had not sought the appointment; it was the Mayor who made the decision. Apparently he had been told not to appoint Mr. Manuel Ramos because he had badmouthed Lindsay when he was helping Mario Procaccino run for Mayor. It was during those conversations that my name came up. At any rate, I took the job as Criminal Court Judge and started on October 3, 1969. Little did I know it would become my life's vocation and that I would decide to stay in the judiciary. I had to sell two of the three cars I had, reduce our standard of living and adjust to my new work and income.

I was assigned to New York Criminal Court and started in the Bronx where I remained until 1975. Manny Gomez was in Manhattan and I was the first and only Puerto Rican judge in the Bronx. I had no problem doing the work, I loved it. Judges enjoy tremendous power, not only in setting bail but also in sentencing and in extending consideration to people who appear before you them. My motto was then, as it is now, to treat people with decency, respect and give them their day in court. I had no problems dealing with defendants who appeared before me nor with their attorneys, whom I would always treat well. I had not forgotten how badly I was treated by some judges and decided that if I became a judge, I would not do that.

At the time, criminal court judges tried misdemeanor cases, that is, cases of drugs, policy, assaults and the like, misdemeanors were the maximum you could receive was one year in prison. The court calendars were very crowded and plea bargaining covered most cases. In plea bargaining, people agree to plead guilty in return for lesser sentences. As many as 95% of the cases in the criminal justice system are resolved by plea bargaining. I believe that I tried maybe five to six percent of the cases that were sent to me. In addition to that I handled arraignments for the court, bails and the like and somehow I still managed to get some trial experience. I began to enjoy being a judge. That is not to say that there were not problems. For one thing I did not allow the court officers to run my court. I was disturbed by the fact that most of judges were not interested in working and would pass the buck as often as possible. Since they were named by the Mayor for definite terms, there was nothing that could be done to them whether or not they worked diligently. There were real questions about the competency of some of the judges and whether they favored defendants, the prosecution or some of the attorneys that appeared before them. Occasionally, some controversy erupted over the matter of bail in a case or whether cases were being steered to particular judges or hearing judges or how judges were placed to work in particular parts: gambling, youth, arraignment and trial.

I often incurred the enmity of the D.A.'s Office because I did not follow their requests for bail. I believed on presumption of innocence in the setting of bail and would make a decision after looking at the person's background, whether they would appear in court and not on the whim of the DA's. I was criticized by my colleagues for this, but I told them that since I was the judge I would set bail and do my own sentencing, taking my time and reading the investigation and sentencing report. I also made some decisions that were not considered prosecution oriented. I was labeled a defendant's judge simply because I acquitted several defendants. The criminal justice system is such that if you don't rule for the prosecution each and every time out,

then you are a defendants' judge. I also insisted on
keeping an open mind and giving people their day in
court. I gave people what they were entitled to in a
court of law; a hearing, a motion or trial. I did not
twist anyone's arm to plead guilty, I did not engage
in playing any games and I did not believe that my
job was to get as many dispositions as I could, but
rather to dispense justice. I attempted to be fair and
remain objective, but often that is not what is
expected. I believe that while I consider myself a
fair and impartial judge, I was considered a
defendant's judge and partly because I was a
minority and because I acquitted a certain number
of defendants. Despite run-ins with the D.A.'s,
Office I found that some prosecutors were regular
people, interested in justice as I was.

Police brutality posed a serious problem.
These were cases where the police officer would
rough up the defendant; break their legs and arms
and then charge the defendant with additional
charges of assault on the officer. They would also
charge them with interference with the
governmental administration of justice, assault and a
laundry list of charges. Generally, the police officer
did not appear at arraignments, claiming they were
out sick and the DA would ask for high bail. If the
case were put over, the DA would proceed to have
the defendant indicted before hearing and forfeit

having a preliminary hearing on the matter. On occasions where charges were reduced to simple assault and the cops at trial would not appear in court as complainants to avoid a hearing on these charges. I had three trials in which I acquitted three defendants after trial. One case was so egregious that I directed that minutes be submitted to the Police Commissioner because I believed that police officers were the proper defendants in the case and not those people charged.

It was no wonder that the time came when I had a police brutality case before me, a case of assault by the police on defendants and on the day of the trial, I had, a "sea of blue," cops in uniform, in my courtroom. A motion was made to have me recuse myself on the ground that I could not judge the case fairly because I had acquitted the three previous cases of police brutality before me. I responded that I made judgments on each separate case, considering the facts in each case and invited the people to respond. I asked the defense attorneys if they had any objections to my being on the case. I then pointed out to the prosecution that I was surprised by their motion because if they had done their homework, they would have found out that I was a former police officer and that I sat on the Police Retirement Board for several years as a representative of the Mayor and, therefore, they had no reason to challenge my impartiality. They apparently did not know my history and the motion collapsed. We proceeded to try the case and, incidentally, the defendant was acquitted.

In 1974, the criminal courts began to allow jury trials in misdemeanor cases where the defendants faced up to one year in prison. I was transferred to the Bronx County Courthouse to conduct one of these trials before a jury. The parties included ADA Kelly, who is now a legend in the Bronx in the DA's Office, a gung-ho DA and a young man, Julio Brady who represented the Legal Aid Society. The case involved a sale of drugs, two glassine envelopes. There was testimony that a buy took place on the street and was witnessed by cops across the street, almost a block away. There was a question as to the accuracy of the testimony, and after a demonstration in court, a motion was made to take the jury to the scene of the crime. I granted the motion, directed the jurors go to the scene and had police reenact the hearing. When I saw what took place, I could not believe the testimony, but I denied the motion to dismiss and sent it to the jury for their consideration. The young man being accused had no prior record and did not take the stand. He was convicted in less than an hour of deliberations. Mr. Kelly was so happy that he went to speak to the jurors when they were dismissed to ask them how they reached their decision and how they enjoyed the trial. The jurors said that they had acquitted the defendant because they didn't like his lawyer and because the defendant didn't take the stand. This was in direct violation to my instructions that they were not to consider the defendant's failure to take the stand and that the lawyers were not on trial. The jurors were still in the courthouse and I had Mr. Kelly bring them back where I polled each of them and verified why they had convicted the defendant. A motion was made by Mr. Brady and I granted the motion to set aside the verdict and proceeded to dismiss the case. I later learned that I made an error in dismissing the case because the proper thing to have done was to set aside the verdict and set the case down for a new trial. When District Attorney Roberts learned this, he was livid but somehow he never returned the case to the calendar. I suspect this had something to do with the weakness of the testimony and that it involved two glassine envelopes. Later that year I was invited to the Police Academy to lecture on search and seizure and while I was there, I was asked the question, "When a jury convicts a defendant, can a judge somehow set aside the trial and dismiss the charges?" I said no and they said "well, the officers testified that you did." I explained what happened in that case and that was that.

All trials in court were not entirely serious affairs; there were some moments of levity. I had a hearing in Manhattan on a case of indecent exposure where the defendant was alleged to have exposed himself to the complaining witness. The complaining witness needed an interpreter. During testimony the interpreter said the complaining witness was shocked when the defendant started masturbating, except that he called it in Spanish, doing "la paja." To Puerto Ricans "paja" in Spanish is the "straw" and when interpreter said that the defendant was "doing the straw", the whole court broke into laughter. It turned out that the interpreter was not a Puerto Rican versed in the vernacular and he had just given a literal translation of "la paja," and not the fact that to other Latinos it meant masturbation. When this was brought to the attention of the judges and the jurors in the courtroom, everybody laughed. This demonstrated to me that you had to be wary of interpreters since sometimes they had written credentials, but where not familiar with the vernacular and the idioms or the customs of Puerto Ricans, Dominicans and others.

Around the same time, they began to appoint Criminal Court judges as Acting Supreme Court Judges assigned to try cases in Supreme Court. While you did the work of a Supreme Court judge you didn't get the salary, which amounted to about a $3000 difference at the time. At first, I assumed that the judges were chosen to sit in the Supreme Court on merit. I soon realized that the selections were made according to political affiliation and I believe, race, color and creed. At the time there were three Latino judges in the City, two of us in the Bronx, one in Manhattan. I felt that it was time that we had Puerto Rican judges in the other boroughs as well. Puerto Ricans should not only appear in court as defendants but as lawyers and members of the judiciary too. I applied, believing that Puerto Rican judges should be assigned to Manhattan, the Bronx and Queens, to serve the substantial population of Latinos in those counties. In response the Administrative Judge, David Ross, insisted that they did not make their selection based on ethnicity or color, something I knew not to be true since assignments were made for precisely those reasons.

At this stage in my life, I was becoming increasingly involved in the community through the Center for Constitutional Rights and Amnesty International, organizations dedicated to protecting individual rights. I went to Chile, four times and to Argentina, five times when people were jailed without due process. In Argentina alone, fifteen thousand people had disappeared, tragedies of the oppressive regimes in these countries, Pinochet in Chile and Videla in Argentina.

While in the Bronx, some of my decisions did not sit well with the District Attorney's Office or the police, so I was shipped off to a Youth Part, where those who appeared were young men between sixteen and nineteen. I didn't mind the assignment as such, except that I was there for eighteen months without having had a trial or hearing. I began to feel that I was losing the very skills I had gained and since I had I been turned down to become an Acting Supreme Court justice, I decided it was a good time to leave. I would go practice in the area that interested me now, international law. I wanted to be involved in what was happening in the world around me. I wrote a letter to the Administrative Judge saying that I intended to resign in the fall and return to private practice. I told him that I believed that I was not being used to the extent of my capacity and I felt it be best if I left.

Although I gave them three-months' notice, I was surprised when two days after my letter, I was called in and suddenly offered to be assigned Acting Supreme Court judge. The only caveat was that I would be in Manhattan, not the Bronx. Apparently, Mario Merola, the Bronx D.A. objected to me sitting on the Supreme Court in Bronx County. Another

Manhattan judge, Howie Goldfuss was sent to the Bronx and I, in turn, would go to Manhattan. This was no problem for me since I loved Manhattan. My run-ins with Merola were the result of my asserting my independence in setting my own sentences and my own bail, which rankled him, because the D.A.'s felt they ran the courts and not the judges. There was one case in particular where I released a young man who was supposedly charged with robbery. After a hearing I dismissed the case because there was no probable cause to arrest him. That afternoon, the New York papers such as the Daily News, ran a big headline, "Cops drew guns, blew case". Merola, who didn't even know what had happened in the case, immediately called the papers to say that I extended rights of defendants at the expense of the victims. According to him, I "carried the Fourth Amendment too far."

As it happened, the Puerto Rican Bar Association was holding a dinner in my honor that Friday evening. The Mayor and other politicians were scheduled to come, but decided to bow out because of all the publicity in the papers. Despite this, the dinner turned out to be a success. When it was my time to speak, I quoted from one of my favorite poems, "Invictus", proclaiming that "my head was bloodied but unbowed." I also held a press conference with the Riverdale press, where I was invited to speak about the controversial case; which annoyed Merola to no end when he heard about it. I also filed a complaint against Congressman James Scheuer for statements he made to the effect that I should be removed from the bench. I maintained that the representations he made without being present in court, or having any real knowledge of what happened, violated my rights. I also filed a complaint against the District Attorney for going out of the court system to attack me in the papers. That incident was one of the reasons that I agreed to go to New York County.

Sitting in Manhattan was like a breath of fresh air, although I did not have chambers. My chambers, to the extent I had any, were in the Bronx. In Manhattan, I shared the chambers of José (Pepe) Ramos Lopez, one of my colleagues who sat in the Civil Court. It was like a new day for me and I loved working as an Acting Supreme Court Justice, although it did not involve additional pay. It was like a new day for me. I had no problems with the District Attorney Morgenthau's Office and the Legal Aid Society and the private bar seemed to respect me and like me. During those years, the Village Voice ran a yearly article on the ten best judges of New York and for three years, my name was among the ten top state judges who were highly regarded and respected.

I went to New York County in 1975 as an Acting Supreme Court Judge and was placed mainly in trial parts. Within a year, I applied and was selected for a seat on the Supreme Court. Supreme Court justices are elected to the bench, and in 1976, there were five vacancies for the Supreme Court, three in Manhattan and two in the Bronx. Walter Diamond, who had been campaign manager for Herman Badillo, called me up and said "How would you like to be a Supreme Court judge?" Since I had made the decision to stay in the judicial system, I said, "Why not." He said, "I could make you one" and I told him to "be my guest." The first thing he did was schedule a meeting with the Bronx County leader, Patrick Cunningham, whose first reaction when Walter told him he would like me to be the first Puerto Rican Supreme Court justice in the Bronx, was "over my dead body." I was seen as a reformer and they wanted no part of me even though I would have been the first Puerto Rican to be elected to the Bronx Supreme Court. However, I was not deterred. "F*ck them, let's go to Manhattan," I said to Walter, "I think they are more liberal there." Walter followed my advice and scheduled me to appear before a reform Democratic club, the Kostikyan Club in Manhattan.

To run for election to the Supreme Court, you had to be designated by a judicial convention. There was, in those days, a nominating convention that handled Bronx and Manhattan and decided who would run for five seats. The party made the decision, not the individual candidate. During my appearance at the Kostikyan Club, I noticed that there were no brown or black faces in the crowd and yet, to fill the five vacancies, they picked five white candidates three from Manhattan and two from the Bronx, all of Jewish extraction. Fritz Alexander, an African American who was working as an Acting Supreme Court justice, had been designated to the Supreme Court by the Governor and was also interested in being appointed. I looked around the room and said that they apparently were not taking into consideration the representation of Latinos and blacks in both counties and that the idea of naming five white judges was ludicrous, since they already represented about 80% of the judiciary in the Supreme Court. I told them that Fritz and I would have been the first minorities to be considered and they were making a mistake by ignoring the statistics about who sat in the courts in both the Bronx and Manhattan. In fact, justice was not blind and that they should take off the blinders and look at the reality of the situation. I left the meeting saying that they could choose to continue excluding us from being selected to the Supreme

Court, but that the day would come when we would rightfully take the positions from them because justice was on our side.

I understand that after I left, they caucused and the net result was that Fritz and I were included in the reform group of five judges to be selected. It was now up to the judicial convention that was taking place that year. I went to the convention with my son, John, and my two campaign managers. As the convention got rolling, I found out that the regular Democratic leader of the Bronx had forbidden the eighteen Latino club leaders in the Bronx to vote for me. I did manage to get John LoCicero from the Village Independent Democrats and the people from Co-op City to decide to throw their vote for me. After two hours of jockeying back and forth everything came to a standstill because each side was short by three votes. The Bronx Democratic organization sent for me and I met with and Paul Victor and George Miller who represented the regular Democratic club. Before I went up to meet with the regulars, who had made every attempt to get Lou Gigante, a Catholic priest who was supposed to be the champion of the Puerto Ricans, to back me. "I thought that you're the champion of the Puerto Ricans," his response was a four-letter-word, to the affect that, "screw the Puerto Ricans", for all he cared. They also tried to enlist the support of Ramon Velez, the big Democratic kingpin of the Bronx. There was one Latino, Democratic assemblyman from Manhattan who was backing me, Angelo Del Toro. They attempted to pressure him to change his support by offering his people seats in the State Senate but he turned them down.

At that meeting I had with George Miller and Paul Victor from the Regular Democratic organization, they said, "look kid, you can't win, we can't win. This is what we are going to do. We are going to give you one of the Bronx nominations and this way you won't have to run because you'll be our candidate." I was surprised at this and said, "Look, a week ago when I went to you, wanting to become your candidate, you said 'over my dead body.' Now you're telling me that I could have the nomination." They said, "Well what do you care? You have it now. You'll be the only guy who walks in there knowing he has the nomination in his pocket." I told them, "Look, that may very well be but I came here with the reform people, as their candidate, to run against you, the regulars, and now you are telling me to turn against them, which would deprive them of a judgeship. "Those people treated me well and if it weren't for them I wouldn't be here. Not only that, downstairs are my two campaign managers and my son. I never expected to win this, I am a reformer. They have never won and you are telling me that the only way I could win this seat is by selling them out. I don't want to." When they responded by asking "What do you care, once you got it, it's in your pocket?" I said that I did care, "if this is the only way I can get it, you can take this job and shove it up your @ss!" and I walked out. I believe that was important in getting the nomination.

After a two hour delay, the matter finally went to a vote. My name was put first and Alexander second. We wound up trouncing the regular organization, winning by 111 to 87. This signaled the end of regular and reform meetings together. Our meeting broke the damn and you would no longer have to negotiate with the regular organization. The reformers could run on their own. The Democratic Regular 12th Judicial District was created to handle the Bronx only. As a result of that, other Puerto Ricans became judges, namely Edwin Torres and Carmen Ciparick, were nominated and won. Ironically, at my induction many of those Puerto Rican leaders who had failed to vote for me, were there congratulating me and slapping me on the back. When I got up to speak, I called them a bunch of "*come mierdas*," literally "sh!t eaters" loosely translated as hypocrites. I knew that they had all been forbidden to vote for me, but I reminded them that blood is thicker than water. In the end, I was elected by strangers, people from Co-op City, non Puerto Ricans delegates and people from the Village. Mike Dontzin was quite surprised by my speech. He told me, "Jesus Christ Carro, how could you do that? You just told all those people what you thought of them." I responded, "It serves them right, Mike. Don't worry about it. I just won a fourteen-year term. I doubt they'll be around fourteen years from now to criticize what I do, besides, by that time I'll probably be eligible for a retirement pension so it doesn't worry me." And thus I became a Supreme Court Justice from the Bronx, the first Puerto Rican to be elected from the Bronx.

In the Supreme Court, I sat mostly in trial parts. The last year I was there, I was placed in a long-term detainee part for people who had been in prison over one year and were still waiting for trial. Those cases generally could not be negotiated by pleas and were strictly trials- it seems the longer a person is in prison, the more innocent he feels. Of the last forty cases I handled, thirty-five were homicides, hence I got tremendous experience trying cases. Because of this my record in the Supreme Court proved to be a problem when I decided that I might be interested in going to the

Appellate Court. Whenever I went before a committee that reviewed the candidates' applications to the Appellate Division of Supreme Court, I would be turned down, because I had a great deal of criminal experience but no civil experience. Telling them that very few judges where considered for criminal trials. I told that if I tried a murder case, I felt I could try any case, did not help. When a judicial friend of mine from the Bronx, Leo Milonas became Administrative Judge of the Civil Part, I went to see him. I said, "Leo, you have to get me some civil experience. Every time I get interviewed for a job, I get turned down because I have only criminal experience, no civil experience. I have to get me some." Leo promised to do something about it and the next thing I knew I was assigned to the Civil Part, where in the first month, I handled several thousand motions. Civil motions came in by the hundreds, so much so, that I had to be assigned two additional assistants to help me and my law secretary, George Levine to handle them. I tried several civil cases, one of them, with the top civil lawyer, who had more million dollar civil verdicts than any lawyer I know. I discovered that trying civil cases was much easier. First, jury selection did not take anywhere near as long. Judges generally selected the civil juries in a day or so, whereas in criminal cases, they could take a week, and second, the charge that you give to jurors in a civil case care is far simpler than that which judges give in criminal cases. In civil cases, juries do not deliberate for days on end. It is simpler for judges to handle civil cases as opposed to criminal cases where judges have to impose, what some people consider, draconian sentences. At any rate, Milonas was able to accommodate me and I did get some civil experience under my belt.

The federal court was not much different than New York State regarding the absence of Puerto Rican and Latino judges. In 1989, while I was still in the Appellate Division, the federal judiciary still had no judges in New York in federal judiciary. In the district court, Judge Jose Cabranes, who was named by Senator Abe Ribicoff from Connecticut was the only one. Cabranes was a professor at Yale Law School along with his wife. I attempted to become a judge in the circuit court when President Carter wanted to name a Latino and a black person to the federal courts. At the time I had put my name on a list, along with 250 others which went to the Judicial Nominating headed by Charlie Walsh. President Carter also had Leonard Garment on his chief of staff. I was interviewed by the Federal Judiciary Committee among whom were Judith Kaye, who subsequently became the presiding justice of the Court of Appeals and a Puerto Rican member, Ramon Nora who came from the Governor's Office. Nora, whom I had gotten to know, kept me informed as to my progress in the interview process. During my interview I was asked at the interview why I thought I belonged on the circuit court. I responded that the court had representatives from everywhere, academia, Ivy League, corporate world, but none from the Latino community. I would be the representative of my group. I said that since many of the people who appeared there, were my people, Latinos should be on the bench. Among the candidates being considered at the time, were Constance Baker Motley, an African American judge and I knew that the President was interested in appointing a Latino to the other seat. Because Judge Motley's name was being pushed, my former law partner, Mary Johnston Lowe, also African American, did not apply because she did not want to reduce the chances of Motley being considered. Motley had seniority. Motley's name was one of the 250 names originally submitted, of which eight would be sent to the President and he, in turn, who would name two. I learned that I made it all the way up to number nine, falling just one short of making the group of eight. Apparently, because Mr. Nora did not vote for Motley and in retaliation, my name did not get the votes to come out of committee. Instead, Newman, who was white, and a black woman were reported out of the committee. I received a letter from Charles Walsh, the Chairman of the Committee, saying that the Committee regretted that I was not one the names sent to the President. The members of the Committee wrote a letter on my behalf to Governor Carey and Senator Moynihan saying that they were sorry that I had not been selected, that I belonged on the bench and encouraged submitting my name for consideration to both Moynihan and Carey for appointment to the Appellate Division or Federal District court. Moynihan acknowledged the letter and sent me an application, as did Governor Carey. In the meantime, I decided to visit the federal court and the Appellate Division and to see which I preferred. I had a friend, Larry Pierce, who was a federal judge. During my visit, while waiting around the federal court, I felt like a total stranger. There were few black people and no Latinos in the place and I felt alienated.

In contrast, when I went to the Appellate Division First Department in Manhattan, there were among the judges, people I knew, namely Judges Bloom, Ross, Sullivan from the Bronx, Sandler and Murphy who had been my classmate. The Appellate Division First Department had jurisdiction over Manhattan and the Bronx. I decided I would most likely be happier in the Appellate Division, where my former colleagues were and where I would deal with people from Bronx and Manhattan. I would be among friends, sitting on cases of my people from Bronx and Manhattan and I felt more comfortable that I belonged there. I then applied to state court and not to federal court at the time. It took three attempts before I was named to the Appellate Division First Department. My appointment was largely the result of waging my own campaign in support of the application. I didn't have anyone promoting me. I wrote a single letter to Governor Carey and El Dario Newspaper pointing out that Governor Brown of California had made many Latino appointments to their appellate courts of the judiciary and that it was time that we had representation in New York State appellate judiciary as well. Richard Brown, who was Governor's Counsel at the time, was someone I knew because he had been a member of the Constitutional Convention in 1976 and was a friend. I got in touch with him. He kept me informed as to my standing in the appointment process. He advised me that I was under consideration but it would be a matter of time.

The first time that I was under consideration there was a problem because Mary Anne Krupskaya, a Liberal Party nominee, was under consideration. They ultimately put someone else in that position. The second time, they had a problem with the Liberal Party and it was decided to appoint Max Bloom, who was backed by the Liberal Party. Richard Brown told me not to worry about that because Bloom was one year away from retirement and his appointment would most likely be for a year. The third time a vacancy occurred when, Herbert Evans, an African American judge in the First Department, decided to go into private practice and created a position. David Ross was interested in becoming Administrative Judge for the Office of Court Administration (OCA). They did not want him in that position and decided to move him to the Appellate Division instead. Richard said that I would be considered for the next appointment.

Shortly thereafter a vacancy was created when Justice Miles Lane retired from the Appellate Division, First Department. It was then, several months after Dave Ross' appointment, that I got a call from the Governor's Office notifying me that they were appointing me to the Appellate Division; in December 1979, I was the first Puerto Rican judge to so be selected for that position. On the day I received the letter, I was not working and decided to go to the Appellate Division at 27 Madison Avenue, to see about my new position. I had not been there since I had been admitted to practice in 1956. It was 3:00 pm on December 19th or 20th of 1979 and I was dressed on my day off, in a leather jacket, ten-gallon, Stetson cowboy hat and sneakers. When I walked into the basement at 27 Madison Avenue, the clerk said to me, "Deliveries are through the rear." I mentioned to him I was the new judge. His jaw sagged but he quickly got his composure and welcomed me aboard. Among the first to welcome me there was Judge Joe Sullivan who said they were happy to have me there and that he was sure I would love the job and feel at home. Well, I did feel at home among my colleagues, including Judge Leo Milonas, who said that this was the greatest job in the world.

I wish I could say that tremendous progress has been made in bringing diversity to the judiciary. I was the first Puerto Rican judge to be appointed to the Appellate Division, where I remained the only Puerto Rican for 16 years. Upon the leaving after 16 years, I thought I had created Puerto Rican seat, as Thurgood Marshall had created a seat on the Supreme Court. Instead and Italian-American was appointed after me It was not until 8 years later that we had another Puerto Rican there.

Chapter Nine
Education and the Law

While still working as a sitting judge in the Criminal Court, I decided to pursue teaching, something I had always had an interest in. With the encouragement of Frank Bonilla who was the Director of the Center for Puerto Rican Studies at City College, I began by taking a course there. The course was entitled, "Perspectives on Justice", and after a series of lectures given by me and others, I was invited to speak to the class. Among the guest lecturers were people who could speak knowledgeably about the criminal justice system: lawyers, prosecutors, police officers, correction officers, and inmates. The course consisted of approximately twelve lectures, two hours each, where the speakers discussed their roles in the criminal justice system as viewed from their perspective. Probation officers, police officers, correction officers, and inmates would give their particular view of the part they played and the impact they had on people around them. The course was well attended and I am greatly indebted to those who participated.

Whetted by the experience at the Centro, I decided that the college community needed to be educated about the criminal justice system and its impact on those who appeared before it. I drew up an outline on a course entitled, "The Criminal Justice System and the Poor." It was designed to show how the system deals with the poor, from a plain stop by a police officer to questions, arrest, bail and court appearances, right through to trial and sentence. The course would address the rights of those caught up in the system with a step by step solution. I applied for a position at the Puerto Rican Studies Department of City College and was made an adjunct professor. I was hired by Professor Frederica Aquino Bermudez to teach at City College.

I taught there for approximately ten years, from 1972 to 1983. I scheduled classes around my duties in Criminal Court, generally from 8:00 to 9:00 am and 7:00 to 9:00 pm, once or twice a week. When I had night duty in court, the class would come to the court and help process cases. I used the court calendar to show the students how the process functioned in reality, from arraignment to setting bail. I would often invite students to sit with me at the bench and observe the proceedings. At recess, we would discuss aspects of some of the pending cases; the nature of the charges, what bail should be set and how they felt the attorneys had comported themselves. It was funny to see that in many instances and after the initial hesitancy, the students wound up thinking that they could do as well as lawyers in arguing before the court.

This was a new experience for the students and when it came to reviewing the setting of bail, I found them to be quite conservative and not at all inclined to release many of these people on their own recognizance or to give them light bail. I was compelled to tell them that the people we were arraigning were poor, and if we set bail that they could not make, they would languish in jail until their next court appearance. Since bail is made to ensure that people return to court, you have to take into consideration the background and the likelihood that they would return. I emphasized that many of the people who appeared could not give you the skin of a grape and in setting bail that is too high, we are upsetting the presumption of innocence. For those who were jailed because they could not get bail, judges were less likely to think of releasing them on parole- someone who comes out from behind bars. On the other hand, if you make bail, your lawyer can arrange for you to come to court dressed up, tell you what to expect and attempt to get you to do something worthwhile when you are out on bail, which makes it more difficult for the court to revoke your bail or to set a high bail or get acquitted at trial.

My experience as a judge was that judges took notice whether someone comes from the audience or from behind bars and they are not likely to think twice letting someone stay in while the case proceeds. When you are out on bail you can always try to find a job, giving your lawyer something to hang his hat on when you return and also to prepare for trial by seeking witnesses. Hence, making bail is quite consequential to the outcome of your case.

One of the high points of the course was a visit to Riker's Island Prison. As was the case with the public at large, I was amazed by how little many of these students knew about the criminal justice system. They had never been inside a prison and their misconceptions about how different they thought they were from those who committed crimes. With these visits I succeeded in showing them that people in jail where just the same as people out of jail, the only real difference being that they got caught at whatever it is that they were doing. The visit to Riker's was very enlightening because it dispelled many of those notions and sparked an interest in wanting to help these people.

The course was also a benefit to me, since it exposed for me the attitudes of ordinary people about the role of the court. The course was successful and brought about the opportunity to teach at Lehman College, Staten Island Community College and at night at Fordham University. One may ask why I decided to teach at the college level rather than law school. I was invited to teach at Rutgers Law School. I chose not to because in college I would be able to teach many of these students in the Puerto Rican Studies Departments and similar programs. In law school, the students are already committed to becoming lawyers. However, at the college level, I hoped I could inspire them, first, to stay in school and perhaps, after seeing lawyers function in the courtroom and studying the material I provided, they could decide to become lawyers on an informed basis.

It was at this time I, along with Dr. Frank Bonilla and Hostos Community College, as well as State Senator Bob Garcia, advanced the idea of giving inmates from Greenhaven Prison access to the college experience. They would be released to attend college since it was my feeling that the college experience is not merely going to college but also being on the campus and meeting fellow students. It was agreed that we would conduct an experimental program, in conjunction with the Legislature through Senator Garcia and the college, and the Center for Puerto Rican Studies. I would visit Greenhaven Prison, select a number of students there who showed an interest in this course, who were safe enough to be taken into the program and to have them transferred from Greenhaven Prison to Sing Sing Prison which is the nearest prison in the state to Hostos Community College in the Bronx. They would be bussed daily from the prison to classes and back to the prison. Although the idea was for me to make the selection of students to participate, lo and behold when I went to Greenhaven Prison, I found that the Warden had already selected the people he felt should take part. I was annoyed by this but was unable to contact Senator Garcia in Albany, so the Warden was able to prevail upon them that it was his prerogative to make the selection and, consequently, we had to go along with that. He selected the participants and then arranged for prisoners selected to be transferred to Sing Sing Prison and thereafter, to attend Hostos Community College.

At first, the program appeared to go along smoothly and showed great promise. It confirmed my belief that the experience of being at the college and attending regular classes with other students was much different than having a teacher go to the prison to teach the prisoners. Soon, however, problems began to arise. For one neither the regular inmates at Sing Sing or Greenhaven were too happy with the idea that fellow inmates, were now being released to attend college on the Bronx campus of

Hostos Community College. The Warden and the Department of Corrections were not happy with the additional problem of bussing the inmates back and forth. The corrections system viewed its key responsibility as security not education. The Warden grew impatient with the problems that arose in the general population at Sing Sing and the program was halted and put it back at the Greenhaven Prison. We had to agree to this and much to my chagrin, the program continued with the understanding that if we wished, we could continue teaching but only at Greenhaven Prison. It became my job to go to Greenhaven Prison once a week and teach the courses there. Even this became problematic because often the inmates could not be located and couldn't come to class. Corrections made no effort to cooperate and, in fact, on several occasions the classes were not ready when I arrived. Ultimately we had to stop the program, which saddened me because I believe the students were getting a great deal from it and were enjoying the experience.

The authorities were more concerned with security than education and felt that if the inmates wanted education, they should receive it within the confines of the prison. This was not just true of my program but also representative of the attitude towards educating prisoners in general. This is very short-sighted because the lack of education is precisely one of the reasons that people end up in prison. Most of the inmates are school dropouts who often have severe learning disabilities. Investing in programs that would prepare them to participate in society would be possible with basic education and some vocational counseling.

One of the many gifts that my mother gave me was a strong belief in the importance of education. That belief has made me a life-long learner and I have always sought out new educational experiences. Early in my career, while working in the Mayor's Office, employees were invited to participate in the NYU School of Public Administration's Executive Program. In 1963, I attended the program that lasted several weeks. I found the program quite interesting. As a result of my participation NYU offered a master's credit for J.D.'s with the understanding that I would pursue a Ph.D. in Public Administration. After considering the offer, I concluded that Ph.D.'s are for those who want to specialize in a given field and that my interests did not lie in the field of public administration; I was interested in trial work. I reluctantly turned down the invitation and settled with the certificate that the program awarded.

**Mayor Robert Wagner, Mom and I
at my Swearing-In as Assistant to the Mayor**

Later in my life, as a judge, I seized every opportunity that I was offered to avail myself of any available educational opportunities for members of the bench. One such program was the National Trial Judges' Program, which was located in Reno, Nevada. I applied to go to the basic program and was selected. I was given a grant to attend so that neither I nor the State of New York had to pay out of pocket for it. The basic program lasted about four weeks. The only sacrifice I made to attend was the use of my vacation time. Because of the grant, I was able to bring my wife and my children to Nevada. There I met judges from all other states and I was able to learn about how other states dealt with the problems we had in New York, that is, issues of sentencing, probation and the effects of drug use.

I enjoyed the basic program so much that I followed up with taking part in all the programs that were given. I took the advanced program, the sentencing program, and the graduate program. Each time I took a class, I managed to have my expenses paid for because there were so few minority judges in the United States and they welcomed having a Puerto Rican judge participate. I was particularly happy to take the sentencing program were I met with judges from Mississippi and other states. We often found the regional differences amusing. In one class we were asked "how long did it take you to sentence somebody?" Most of the attendees replied that it took about thirty minutes. When it came down to me I said that it takes me two minutes. This prompted the judge from Louisiana to say "Hell, Carro, you ain't got no justice in New York." My response was "look who's talking." I said that sentencing takes me two minutes to make it clear that I review the investigation and sentencing reports beforehand. I would take a recess to read them and take notes on them before I actually engaged in sentencing. I always gave the attorneys an opportunity to proceed and submit briefs on behalf of their client. If they wished, the defendant could speak on his own.

After a while, New York State no longer allowed its judges to attend the National College of Judiciary in Nevada and a program in-state was created in New York. The out-of-state programs proved to be a great experience for me, not only did I meet judges from California and other jurisdictions including Puerto Rico. I formed lasting friendships with people whom I am always able to call upon when I travelled.

As part of the Nevada program, there was an experiment that involved a number of judges who would spend the night in a Nevada prison. Fifteen of us volunteered and arranged to spend the night in a prison, without the inmates knowing we were there. While there, as bedtime came, I noted that many of the prisoners talked, some in their sleep, and disrupted the others. This was not a good situation and I wondered what it was like to be there for a long period of time with no thought of coming out. In the midst of this, at about midnight, it was learned that there were judges taking part in the program. When the word got out to the inmates, the experiment was called off. It was unfortunate because I wanted to see how it turned out. The next day, when I was asked about it, I said that it was a harrowing experience for those who took part. This was different from the ordinary visits where judges are required to visit prison once a year, meet with the Warden, have lunch and there is just time for a cursory visit. This was different in that we were actually put in cells with the inmates and in my opinion, it was so harrowing that I said in an interview, that I felt that they should "bulldoze the f*cking place."

In 1980, I learned that the University of Virginia Law School had a program where you could get a master's degree in judicial process. There was a special program for judges who were admitted from all jurisdictions, federal and state. As usual, I could not afford the tuition but I applied for a scholarship which was granted. I was one of thirty invited to participate in a program which would lead to a master's after attending two summers in 1980 and 1981, then taking one year to write a thesis. Compared to my law school years this was an idyllic experience. I had attended Brooklyn Law School at night, commuting back and forth in the subway. Only when I was given a fellowship was I able to switch to days, still commuting back and forth, but in a Volkswagen rather than the subway. I did not know what it was to attend a school such as the University of Virginia, established by Thomas Jefferson in 1806, who had a personal hand in designing the architecture. It has over 2,000 acres and persons such as Edgar Allen Poe, Ralph Sampson, the basketball player, Bobby Kennedy, Ted Kennedy among its illustrious alumni. It is a state school with a law school, a business school and medical school that are all among the top 25 of such institutions in the country. There are nine different categories for different degree programs. When I graduated, the graduating class was over 1000 students and the ceremony was held outside in the quadrangle; it was something to behold. I was fortunate to participate in the program with some of my former classmates of mine, including Joseph Sullivan, my colleague from the NYS Appellate Division, First Department and Larry Bracken from the Second Department, who I saw regularly while there. I also met a federal judge Juan Torruellas, from the District Court of Puerto Rico, along with judges from Louisiana, California, Georgia and Florida.

My scholarship included tuition, room and board and transportation for my entire family. My wife, and initially some of my children, came with me and we were given a three-bedroom, air conditioned apartment on the grounds of UVA. In addition to the apartment, I received $25.00 a day for food, on which we managed nicely.

We took courses from nine to five which were not esoteric or exciting, however, they considered law from an economic perspective. I had not studied law in this way before. The methodology was influenced by the work of professors from the University of Chicago Law School. As an example in one of the final exams I was asked to take a legal decision and turn it into an economic decision. I thought I was having a difficult time enough with doing the legal aspect without having to turn to economics. One of the courses was taught by a professor of economics, who in tandem with another lawyer, taught the class. Most of the courses were taught this way and it gave us the opportunity, to discuss the common law, medicine and the law and other aspects of the law that I was not familiar with. My wife, who came with me, thoroughly enjoyed the experience. She found the people of Virginia to be very friendly and genteel. The nights were cool and we enjoyed our weekends when we would occasionally get together with my fellow judges and judges from other jurisdictions. Most of time, however, was spent in study and class. It was a heavy schedule and I averaged three or four hours of homework each night plus exams, which were either open or closed book. In either case, they were tough exams, designed to test your mettle. Often, the other Puerto Rican judge attending, Torruellas, and I kidded each other about our performance; he would ask, "John, what if we failed this course, can we face our people who would die at the thought of it?" I also enjoyed some social time with Joe Sullivan, who was there without his wife. He invited us for breakfast one morning and made scrambled eggs. Unfortunately while making the eggs, he put a plastic fork in the pan and it melted into the food. Also, while doing laundry, he put soap in the dryer which caused a conflagration. He was embarrassed and asked, "Please don't tell my colleagues about this when we get back to court. I'll never hear the end of it." I made the promise and kept my solemn oath.

After attending classes for two summers, we had to select a master's thesis topic and the topic had to be approved. My first choice for a topic had already been selected and I was asked to write on something else. I discovered a new topic. However the University of Virginia, despite having a fantastic library with over 750,000 volumes, had little about the study of law in Cuba, particularly since the Castro revolution. Since I spoke Spanish, the University suggested that my thesis topic should be focused on the legal education system of Cuba in the wake of becoming a Communist/Socialist country, converting from the English legal system to the French. In my studies at the law school, I concentrated on examining the judicial processes that constituted the American, the English, the French and the German systems; the University was interested in looking at the influence of Communism on the legal systems of Cuba and Russia among other countries.

I agreed to do it, but discovered that the logistics were more difficult than I imagined. I needed permission to travel to Cuba and I would have to go there when the courts were open, which generally was not during the summer. I was able to get time off from my court system to go to Cuba and to obtain State Department clearances to travel there for judicial purposes. I managed to stay three weeks in Cuba in 1983. In Cuba, I found that they were generally aware of my request to study the legal system and were most cooperative. They made no effort to restrict what I did and how I did it. I was able to visit two law schools, one in the capital, Havana, and the other in Santiago. The visit to Santiago was particularly interesting because it is where Castro started the revolution. It was the site of the Sierra Maestra Mountains from which the revolution began and there were museums dedicated to that part of Cuban history. I learned about Castro's imprisonment at the Moncada Barracks and the events he described in his book, "History Will Absolve Me." I was given a copy.

In the US, we are generally not aware that Cuba is one of the most advanced countries of Latin America. It is thirteen times the size of Puerto Rico and has a population of over 10 million people. Cubans are known as the "Jews" of Latin America. They are very enterprising and very good in all fields. They are not stereotypically only good in sports. It seems to be the only country with better boxers (and baseball players) than America. If they had taller basketball players, they would probably give us a run for our money in that sport too. While there is interest in sports, I found the Cuban system provides for the education of young people who have the ability but who are poor. I learned that Cuba advanced before Castro's revolution, when over ninety per cent of the lawyers fled because they had been part of the influential ruling class. The laws that existed before the revolution were abolished. Apparently Castro felt at the time, that lawyers, he could do without. He learned, that with respect to negotiating treaties with other countries, that lawyers were a "necessary evil".

My research indicated there were seven lawyers left in Cuba. Most had migrated to the United States and settled largely in Florida. When Castro realized that he needed lawyers, he reopened the law schools and made it a priority to develop lawyers. The law practiced in Cuba however had to be consistent with the Communist system. There were no private law firms and the corporate law practice did not exist. Lawyers did not practice capitalist law, where they would be required to work for and to serve the people in the manner of a government sponsored, legal aid practice. There were no millionaires or financial giants of Cuba, rather, professionals like doctors and lawyers, from among the people, to serve the people.

For my research, I was able speak to students at both the law schools, to visit the courts and some of the nearby prisons. I was given free latitude to speak to anyone and was not censored in any way. I learned a great deal about how Cuban society and its economic system functioned. For example, in Cuba your rent could not be more than ten per cent of your income. All education and healthcare was free. True, there was not the freedom of speech that exists in the US. The trade off is providing rent regulation, free education and health care; these and other programs would virtually eliminate poverty, as we know it there.

The educational system was especially interesting. Every school was given 250 to 500 acres, on which the students were taught to farm their own products, making the school self sufficient in providing food for their student body and the local people. Everyone participates in the harvests, such as the coffee harvest. No distinction exists between professionals such as lawyers and engineers, and ordinary people. Everybody is a "compañero or compañera," a companion. It was my observation that there seemed to be no racism in Cuba. This was confirmed for me when I met Huey Newton, the former Black Panther, and his wife Gwen who had fled to Cuba. Over lunch, he said to me that of all the places he had been to, Cuba was the most free in terms of racial attitudes and equality of men and women.

I returned from Cuba armed with several weeks of research and spent several months at home putting it together for my thesis. In the end, I wrote a thesis entitled, "The Structure, Legal, Education and the Practice of Law in Socialist Cuba." The thesis was approved and I received a master's degree in Comparative Law in 1984. My thesis was published by the University of Virginia Law School in 1984. It was also published by Catholic University Law School Law Review in Ponce, Puerto Rico in the July-October 1985 edition.

My Best Friend, Dr. Frank Bonilla

Chapter Ten
Serving the Public in Other Ways

In 1972, I received a telephone call from the Office of the Secretary of Defense, Melvin Laird, in Washington D.C., during which I was asked if I was willing to participate in a task force designated by President Nixon, under the aegis of Secretary Laird designed to look at racism in the Administration of Military Justice in the armed forces of the United States and throughout the World. I agreed to participate and indicated that I was willing and was told that for this purpose the Pentagon would ask the Office of Court Administration for the City of New York to give me a leave of absence to serve on this task force. I was cleared by the court to participate and was granted a one-year leave.

The task force consisted of thirteen people selected by Secretary Laird, including the Judge Advocates General of the four branches of the military- the Army, Navy, Air Force and Marine Corps, as well as some federal judges and other civilians from Washington and elsewhere. Along with me, some of the civilian members were Haywood Burns, a prominent African American civil rights attorney and professor of law and who later would become the first African American dean of City University of New York Law School, a circuit court judge from Ohio, and Joe Howard, a circuit judge from Baltimore who was African American. As a result of this experience Judge Howard, Haywood Burns and I would become lifelong friends.

HAYWOOD BURNS - CUNY LAW SCHOOL

The task force was to investigate the incidence of racism in the military forces around the world. The members would visit installations, interview personnel, look at the role of the Court of Military Justice, conduct hearings and report their findings. It was created in response to complaints by the Congressional Black Caucus that African-

American soldiers having difficulty getting off-base housing in Alaska and Germany. President Nixon, rather than just limit African-American troops, decided this task force would include Hispanics and other minorities and the task force was designated to look into these complaints, also to look at the disproportionate nature of sentences meted out to whites and blacks in the military, often in the same charges for the same cases. Furthermore, how minorities fared in the armed services in general.

I was assigned to Far East and visited the Philippines, Okinawa, Japan and bases out there such as Subic Bay. Before we traveled abroad we attended an orientation at the Pentagon about the makeup of the armed forces. The lectures were given by a black military man and future general and we learned a great deal about what was being done in the Marine Corps, the Army, and the Navy to see that blacks were well represented and who, for example, would be the first African American to become a Marine Corps. General. The military had difficulty in classifying Latinos. They would list us as Spanish Surnamed Americans but did not divide Puerto Ricans, Cubans or Mexicans and did not where to place us as to race, since Latinos could be white or black. They were wholly not equipped to identify us, although there is a substantial number of Latinos in the armed forces. When the lecture ended, I raised my hand and naively asked if they knew who would be the first Puerto Rican or Latino general in the armed forces. To my great surprise they explained that they were having problems categorizing us, sometimes we were Spanish-surnamed, other times we were non-white, Spanish-speaking. If they could not even classify us, I harbored little hope that we would see a Latino general anytime soon.

During our visits we conducted interviews, spoke to servicemen and analyzed how the court martial manual was applied with respect to the ethnicity of the soldiers. The task force first looked at military installations in the continental United States with visits to Fort Dix, Camp Pendleton, in the Marine Corps, and several other areas throughout the United States. We then proceeded to divide the task force in half so that half of us would visit the Pacific and half would go to Europe (to existing installations there) and conduct meetings and examinations of military procedures and review how minorities fare in the military, and also look at the Court of Military Justice.

To participate in this, the head of the task force was a three-star general Judge Advocate from the Army, as well as Judge Advocates from the Navy, Air Force and Marine Corps. We had civilian counterparts and in order to facilitate our work as civilian members of the task force, we were given equivalent military ranks; so for example, the judge from Ohio got a three-star general military rank, the same as the head military member of the task force and so forth. Justice Howard, the federal judge, received a two-star general equivalent rank and Haywood Burns and I received one-star general equivalent military ranks. This was a surprise to me because when I was in the Navy, I was a pharmacist's mate, third class which is as far as I had risen and here I was elevated to rank of general to conduct the study. Not only that, but the members of the task force were given diplomatic passports and an itinerary developed to visit the various installations. We were also provided military chauffeurs, a limo with a flag, in addition to the rank of one-star general.

Our group began by going to the Philippines. We visited Clark Air Force Base and were scheduled to go to Subic Bay. We ended up being prevented by the weather. We seemed to be in the middle of a monsoon and it had been raining for twelve consecutive days and had to limit our visit to Clark where we interviewed the men of that facility. On this trip, I became well acquainted with Haywood Burns and we generally worked as a team and became good friends.

We completed the study after twelve months and wrote a report which was published. Our study concluded that racism was systemic and endemic in the military just as it is in civilian life. However, the military was in a position to make changes quickly because they could make changes by fiat or command. In civilian life you could not eradicate racism by simply ordering it to happen. In the military, once the command goes down it is adhered to. This became the majority report with the dissenting opinion by two Judge Advocates. We were invited to present our report to the New York Bar Association, and to two of the Judge Advocate Generals. Professor Burns and I made the presentation. At the end of the presentation, the moderator thanked Professor Burns and I for the fine presentation "despite" the fact that we were minorities. Professor Burns responded, "...we thank the moderator "despite" his racist remark..." This got a big round of applause.

My travelling status for the task force gave me the opportunity to visit Frank Bonilla in Palo Alto, where he was a professor at Stanford. While I was happy to see my friend, there was an ulterior motive for my visit. The newly created Center for Puerto Rican Studies in New York needed a Director and I was determined to convince Frank to take the job. I told him how impressed I was with Stanford and how well he was doing as a tenured professor in Palo Alto. But, I said, he was needed by the Puerto Rican community back East. He was our leading intellectual, and as far I could see in Palo Alto, there were few Puerto Ricans there. I don't know how, but I finally prevailed on him- to give it his consideration and to agree- to take the job of Director of Puerto Rican Studies at City College. He moved his family to New York and bought a home on 116th St. and First Avenue in the middle of the Barrio, which was a strange place for two children coming from Palo Alto. He never looked back, and in fact, he and his children adjusted well. Tony, his son, began taking conga drum lessons in Harlem and going to one of our top public schools, Stuyvesant High School. I think that the only casualty was his wife Tamara, who loved Palo Alto. She felt increasingly left out as a result of Frank's involvement in the Latino community. I believe this in part, led to their estrangement and divorce, something that grieved me deeply because she had become me and my wife's best friend. It was Tamara who helped my wife when one of our daughters was born in Yonkers. Tamara came to our house and stayed for a week. She did not let Teresa get out of bed and she did the entire household chores, took care of the children and she was just so great that we became so fond of her. She has been a true friend, so much so, that when

Frank subsequently remarried, Teresa would not even visit his new wife. I had to prevail on her, saying that Frank's children were accepting the new wife and that because he was my best friend, I had to accept the new wife and so should she. She finally went to visit Frank and meet his wife, something she had refused to do until then. They had a place in Montauk and we were invited often. To this day Teresa is Tamara's best friend and we consider her our best friend.

I also had the unique experience, while a criminal court judge, of traveling to Chile and to Argentina, as part of a task force put together by the Center for Constitutional Rights of New York City, who were very much concerned about the situation in Chile where General Pinochet was incarcerating people and ordering military tribunals instead of civil trials against them, with the possibility of being shot. In Argentina the situation was just as bad. They had these disappearances, where 15,000 people, friends and relatives of the populace had disappeared. As a matter of fact, the mothers of the disappeared used to stage weekly demonstrations outside the "Pink House," Casa Rosada of Argentina complaining to the authorities, General Nidela and his cohorts about the disappeared ones. I was part of the task force who went down there to try to determine what had happened to all these people.

I was fortunate enough to be invited by Columbia University, who was sending a group of approximately thirty to forty people, to visit China with a view towards the education of their mass of people and how they dealt with their health problems. I went to China for a six-week period, twenty-two of us were selected by Columbia University, but we paid for our travel expenses. The group included Frank and several other people I knew well. We flew to Geneva and on to Romania, where a Chinese plane took us to Beijing. At one point I fell asleep and woke up thinking that the plane was losing altitude because I could see the snow-capped mountains. It turned out that the snow-capped mountains were Mount Everest.

Since my retirement I have not had as much time to travel as before, although I was invited to go to Rio de Janeiro in Brazil to take part in a conference of American jurists. There were 103 judges and we went there at the invitation of the Brazilian government. I had the good luck and opportunity to present a paper on the challenges of youth crime, contrasting how we treat our youth here in the United States as compared to other countries. It was a good subject for me. I used the experience of dealing with an eleven-year-old youth who had not committed a crime; he was absent from school and had landed in trouble because of his truancy. I described how I spent a year attempting to help him and his mother- how I thought the situation had been resolved but the mother wanted to leave the jurisdiction, which she did against our wishes- and lo and behold, eleven years later I had looked at papers only to find out that the young boy, Harvey Lee Oswald, had grown up and assassinated President Jack Kennedy on November 22, 1963. I saved this as the last line of the presentation I gave and it proved to be a big hit. My participation was very well received and I was invited to go to other countries including the Dominican Republic and Brazil. While in Brazil I found its culture to be closest to Puerto Rico's. The people are lovely; they love to party, they love to eat, they love to dance and it is just a wonderful country that I hope I will return to one day.

As of writing this, I have spent over fifty years in the practice of law, twenty five in the judiciary and the balance as a private defense attorney. As a result, I think that I have attained enough experience that I can make some observations, in no particular order: the American jury system is our saving grace. It makes us the best justice system in the world that we have. The right to be tried by a jury and the verdict has to be unanimous. There is an axiom I learned in law school. It is far better to be judged by twelve biased sons-of-bitches than by one. Another aspect of our system is that guilt of the defendant must be proved beyond a reasonable doubt by the people; which means, that it is up to the prosecutor to prove your case and the defendant does not have to take the stand or do anything in his defense. He can just sit there and the burden is upon the people. It never shifts as far as proving your guilt. This is contrary to other systems such as the Russian, French and others where the person in question is presumed guilty until proven innocent.

Another tenet of our profession is that you are entitled to reasonable bail, bail that will insure your return to court and you do not have to languish in jail while your case is being tried. This is most important, because, since the law presumes you innocent, you are entitled to be out until your guilt or innocence is determined. As is often the case, some courts will post unreasonable bail and people are made to stay in jail, often for light cases such as misdemeanors. By the time you are tried, you are often maxed out on whatever sentence you would have received. As far as I am concerned, this is a denial of due process. People, particularly the poor, are entitled to a reasonable trial process so they are not prejudged, or become an academic exercise.

There is an important distinction within the Court that made my sixteen years in the Appellate Division unique and extraordinary; namely, it is what other lower courts in New York, (or even the highest State Court- the NY Court of Appeals) are not, i.e, an '*interest of justice jurisdiction*'. This is important because it allows the Court to look at how other courts are handling cases, such as disproportionate sentencing, for the same crime between boroughs, and excessive sentences based on race, color or creed. Having this level playing field allows that justice can be administered fairly and even-handedly. It is only in the Appellate Division that has this type of power, and this attribute makes it unique. An *interest in justice jurisdiction*, allows for reduced sentences, remand for new trials and even dismissals (see People v. Kidd). This is indeed an extraordinary power of the Appellate Division.

Fellow Justices at the Appellate Division First Dept

It is important to note that jurisdictionally, the Court of Appeals reviews issues of law *only*, while the Appellate Division has jurisdiction on both the *law and the facts* of every case.

Oral Arguments at the Appellate Division First Dept

Hence, over ninety percent of cases are heard in the Appellate Division, which looks at the facts and/or the law of the case below, and can do its interest of justice review in these matters, as well as review the adequacy of counsel in the trial below; that is whether the defendant received adequate assistance of counsel. This also serves to preserve the record for appeal by making timely objections.

Fellow Justices in the Conference Room at the Apellate Division 1st Dept

The adequacy of counsel in the court below can be reviewed on appeal *via* NY CPL Section 440 which reviews this matter and can remedy defects, whether or not they have been preserved and appealed in the trial below.

Chapter Eleven
Family

Terri and I married young; she was 17 and I was 19, and our first child, Sherry, was born in 1947. We lived in apartments in the Bronx until our fifth child, Lorna, was born in 1961. In between, we had Christine in 1953, John in 1957 and Greg in 1959. I was then working in Mayor Wagner's Office. When my lease expired, my landlord would not renew so we had to leave and I began to look for a larger apartment. Every day I would look in the New York Times and the New York Post for listings. When I called about renting the apartments, I was asked outright, "What nationality are you?" When I said Puerto Rican, the response was "drop dead" or "get lost," we do not want to rent to you. It was so bad that I had to consider buying a home. We hadn't thought about this before because we didn't have that kind of money, but now I had no choice. At first, I was interested in buying a home in Riverdale or the better sections of the Bronx, but soon realized we could not afford it. We would have to settle for an area where homes did not cost as much and was not too far from where I worked. I was able to find an old, five-bedroom house in South Yonkers, Park Hill, which needed a tremendous amount of repairs. It was selling for $21,000, the cheapest price I could find. We decided to not consider Riverdale or Westchester, although they had great school systems, because the cost was beyond our means. We needed at least $6500 for a down payment to buy the house and I had no money. This is where my old friend Frank came in. He gave me his daughter's bank book, which had $1500 in it. My father loaned us $2000. I was able to make what we call a "serrucho", which means "to saw" and borrow whatever money we could get here and there to make the down payment to get the house. Eventually, we were able to put the $6500 together with loans from my uncle, presents, and the little we had.

The house was old but it had five bedrooms, big enough to accommodate our family even with the addition of Monique in 1961 and Robert in 1968. It was on a hill that we happened to call, "La Jalda". It was sort of like a Spanish house in Puerto Rico called a "quinta" and we grew to love it. It was a very nice neighborhood and only about ten minutes from Court where I worked. The proximity to work was something I would learn later to appreciate (when we moved to Rockland County and I had a long commute and a large gas bill). We did not check out the school system, which proved to be poor. When we first moved there, we were able to send the children to the Catholic schools, but when it was time for high school, paying tuition would become impossible.

We had many good neighbors, among them the Halls, who lived right across the street. Mr. Gus Hall was head of the Communist Party, something we didn't know until we moved there. We were not especially political, and our neighborhood was, in fact, surrounded by Republicans. Another neighbor was Lieutenant Governor Wilson, who eventually became the Governor of the State of New York. He gave me a lift home several times when we both attended official dinners. Another neighbor, Tony

Cerreto, was a Republican leader in Yonkers. The composition of the neighborhood made for funny situations. Gus had built his own sauna, which I was invited to use. It was when I was still Assistant to the Mayor. I can only imagine what would have happened if it ever came out that the Assistant to the Mayor was taking a sauna with the head of the Communist Party at his home. We were relatively innocent in those days and the truth was that Gus Hall and his family were lovely neighbors, as were all the people in the neighborhood, no matter what party they belonged to.

Home in the Library

We lived in Rockland County, the place of our last house, from 1972 until 2002, when all of our children except one were grown and moved away. By 2002, a three-story house with four bedrooms and three heating units had become too expensive for us. We wanted to find a place that was easier to maintain. We moved to where we currently live, in the Retreat at Airmont in Suffern, a complex of six buildings and stores for residents who are fifty-five an older. We are happy here. Our apartment is on the ground floor and we have ample parking under the building. It is an upscale community with a club house and a swimming pool. It is convenient now that we are getting on in age. The complex has many activities for the residents and everything is nearby. There is a Wal-Mart, a Shoprite and a library. I have much more time to spend with my kids and family. My daughter Lorna, who is a pediatrician, lives three minutes away in Monticello. Christine splits her time between the apartment here and Albany, where she works as a law clerk for Judge Carmen Ciparick, a member of the New York Court of Appeals. Our other children have their own home in the City and other places nearby. Sherry is a schoolteacher. John and Robert are attorneys and Monique is a Law Secretary for Supreme Court. John inherited my practice Carro, Carro & Mitchell, specializing in negligence, personal injury and tort cases.

Only Greg, so far, has entered the judiciary. He graduated from Rutgers Law School. Greg expressed an interest in becoming a prosecutor. While working with the Wagner administration, I was assigned to work with Bob Morgenthau, the Manhattan D.A., when he decided to run for Governor. I led his campaign in the Latino community and got to know Bob Morgenthau quite well. He lost the race, but I learned that he was a good guy who was a little stiff and wooden when it came to mixing with crowds in the neighborhood. Given Greg's interest, this proved to be fortuitous. I wrote to Bob Morgenthau who arranged for an interview for Greg. Greg's situation had been an interesting one. He initially did not know what he wanted to do with his life. He took the police exam, and scored a 98% and was going to become a police officer. While waiting to be called, he decided to finish community college in Rockland. When he was called from the list, he declined because he wanted to get his associate's degree. After that, Greg decided he wanted a four-year college degree and applied to Buffalo State. He was accepted, and while attending, he received another call from the Police Department and declined it for a second time. Greg finished Buffalo State, went on to Rutgers Law School and became interested in the D.A.'s Office. I had been told that Mario Merola was interested in having him come to the Office in the Bronx D.A., but I did not think that was a good idea because, at the time, I was on the Appellate Division as an Associate Justice and had, on some occasions, reversed cases from the Bronx because of prosecutorial misconduct. My relationship with Merola had not been that warm and I felt that Greg would do much better if he were to go to Manhattan. I thought it would make for a better situation, because although they regarded me as liberal and pro-defendant, they also respected my decisions. Gregory applied to the Manhattan D.A.'s Office. I wrote to Bob Morgenthau who arranged for an interview with Greg. Greg had his interview with Morgenthau's Office. After the interview, I asked him how it went to which he replied, "Dad you ruined me. You know who else is in that office? John Kennedy, Jr., Dan Rather's and Cyrus Vance's sons", and I said, "So what, they have good people, that is why I sent you there, it's a prestigious office. You're my son, what else is new?" Needless to say, he got the job and he loved it. When he got that job he turned down the Police Department's Office for the third time. He declined the position as a patrolman and became Assistant District Attorney in New York County where he would remain for fourteen years until named as a criminal court judge by Mayor Rudy Giuliani.

In the D.A.'s Office in Manhattan, Gregory worked in Arraignments, the Complaint Bureau, the Trial Bureau and the Rackets and Homicide Bureau. At some point I told him that he should apply for a judgeship. With his experience I thought his chances were good, but Gregory did not agree. He said there were over 400 D.A.s in the Manhattan D.A.'s Office, he was relatively new and he didn't think he would get a judgeship. I told him that the Mayor was interested in having more Latinos as criminal and family court judges and that with his experience he was well qualified. He took my advice and applied.

Gregory's Swearing In Ceremony at Gracie Mansion with Mayor Rudolph Giuliani and Family

When he was named to the Criminal Court it was momentous because the appointment was made by Mayor Giuliani for Criminal Court and then by Governor Pataki to the Supreme Court, who seldom appointed Democrats. At the time, the headline in the New York Times was, "He Won't Follow His Father's Footsteps." The story was written by Dan Wyse who made it a point to say how interesting it was that Giuliani had named the son of John Carro to the bench, because Judge Carro, Associate Justice of the Appellate Division, had a very liberal reputation and was highly regarded by blacks and Latinos, as a "People's Judge." I replied in the article, that Greg was somewhat different from me. He had spent fourteen years in the prosecutor's office and he had a reputation as a more conservative, prosecution-minded judge. I said that I believed it was important to have a person with this point of view on the bench and that we need people in the prosecutor's office who are interested in fair-minded justice. I mentioned that while Gregory was half Puerto Rican and half Italian he was his own man and I counseled him to treat people who appeared before him with respect, dignity and give them their day in court. If he did this he would have no problem with anyone who appeared before him and no one would care about whether his views were conservative or liberal because he would be judged by how he treated defendants in court. I joked that I made a mistake by moving to Yonkers, where he grew up, because it meant he hung out with too many Republicans. My friends got a big kick out of my response which is printed in the New York Times. It spoke very well for Greg that although he was the son of a Democrat and a liberal icon, he was appointed by a Republican Mayor and a Republican Governor.

Greg was subsequently appointed to the Court of Claims, to fill the vacancy created by Dora Irizarry, a Republican Court of Claims Judge, who was picked by Pataki to run on his ticket. Pataki lost and Dora was named to a federal judgeship as a consolation prize. She went on to the federal bench and in the process created a position for Greg in the Court of Claims. I should note that at the time, Pataki, who was running for another term as Governor, was aware that Bloomberg had received 45% of the Latino vote for Mayor, an unprecedented number. In that race, Fernando Ferrer, who was the Democratic candidate for Mayor, lost to Mark Green in the Democratic Primary. Green made the mistake of not reaching out to Ferrer, so the Democrats in the Bronx, where Ferrer was Borough President and Roberto Ramirez was the County leader, sat on their hands. Many Puerto Ricans went on to vote for Bloomberg, who had been smart enough to take lessons in Spanish and court the Latino vote.

This was not lost on Pataki, who decided that he would also make an effort to court the Latino vote. Although he had been in office for eight years he had not appointed any Latinos to the court. There was a vacancy for a Latino justice in all four appellate divisions and yet I spent sixteen years as the only Latino Associate Justice on an appellate court in the State of New York. When he decided to court the Latino vote, he named Luis Gonzalez, someone he had previously rejected two years earlier to the court. At the induction of Luis Gonzalez, Pataki reached out to me and requested that I give him a list of potential Latinos to name to the judiciary. I found this ironic because when I retired from the Appellate Division, First Department in 1994, where I sat for fifteen years and twenty-five years as a judge. I thought that I had established a Puerto Rican seat in the Appellate Division, much like Thurgood Marshall had established a federal seat. Instead of naming another Puerto Rican to take my place, such as Governor Cuomo, he appointed Angela Mazzarelli. For the first time in fifteen years there was no Latino in the Appellate Division. This situation would remain until after Cuomo left office.

In the meantime, Puerto Ricans and Latinos had been recommended to the Governor with no success, Luis Gonzalez, Charles Ramos, Ariel Belen. When Governor Pataki saw that Bloomberg had made inroads into the Latino community he decided to appoint Luis Gonzalez who was then Administrative Judge of the Bronx Supreme Court, to the Appellate Division. At the induction, when Governor Pataki gave me his number and asked me to call him and recommend names for judicial appointments, I told him that I had done so in the past unsuccessfully. I reminded Governor Pataki that I had submitted Ariel Belen, Supreme Court Justice of Kings County for the Appellate Division Second Department. I had personally sent the resume of Ariel Belen to him and had asked Dennis Rivera, President of Local 1199, to recommend him.

After the induction ceremony, I called Governor Pataki but, he wasn't in, so I left my number. Several days later the secretary in my office told me that I had a call from someone named George. I said I didn't know who George was, but asked her to put him on the phone. When he came on the phone, he said "John, this is George." I said, "George who?" He said, "George Pataki". I was so surprised that I said, "Oh, sh!t!" The Governor asked me, "What did you say?" I said, "Oh sh!t, I didn't know which George you were... I know many Georges." I apologized and he laughed. He asked me to submit a few names to him for the consideration of appointment to the bench. I sent the resumes of Ariel Belen and Reynaldo Rivera for the Supreme Court Kings County Appellate Division

and First Department, where we had no
representation. I also sent the name of Gregory
Carro and told him Greg was my son. He was
presently a criminal court judge, named by Giuliani.
He had been a prosecutor for fourteen years and
was outstandingly well qualified to be a Court of
Claims judge. When I told Greg about the
opportunity he didn't think he had much of a
chance since he had already applied for the Court of
Claims through a Republican friend of mine, Eddy
Mercado. Gregory was interviewed but did not get
the job. Instead it went to Dora Irizarry, a
Republican. Nonetheless, Pataki took Greg's name,
along with others I submitted, Reynaldo Rivera and
Ariel Belen.

Gregory's Reception on Becoming a Judge in the Chambers of the Hon. Carmen Ciparick, (J. NY Ct. Appeals)

Several weeks later, Reynaldo Rivera was
named to the Appellate Division Second

Department.   Shortly   thereafter,   Greg   was
interviewed again and on the weekend of Fathers'
Day, I received a call from Governor Pataki's Office
telling me that he was naming my son Greg, to the
bench. I thanked him, and told him that that was
the finest present I could receive for Father's Day.
Greg's name was submitted. He appeared before
the Court and was admitted by the Senate and he
became a Court of Claims Judge. I was able to
accompany him to Albany, where his appointment
was confirmed by the Senate. It was there I met the
Chief Judge of the Court of Claims, Susan Reed,
who was later appointed to the Court of Appeals.
Several months after Greg became a Court of Claims
Judge, Pataki named him an Acting Supreme Court
Judge for Manhattan, which is where he has
remained.

Chapter Twelve
Winding Up

I am often asked how I managed to achieve so many things. I guess an easy explanation has been that I was lucky to be in the right place at the right time. How did a young jíbaro from the mountains of Puerto Rico, fatherless, with no male family models, manage to do all this? I certainly had my share of "firsts" in a community that had just begun to rise. I was the first Assistant to the Mayor in the City of New York's history, the first elected Supreme Court Judge from Bronx County; the first Puerto Rican to serve on New York's second highest Court, the Appellate Division, First Department, where I sat for sixteen years, probably the highest judicial appointment of a Puerto Rican in America at the time. I was a founder of the Puerto Rican Forum, Aspira and the Puerto Rican Legal Defense Fund. I had become the first President of the Hispanic Judges Association and the second president of the Puerto Rican Bar Association. Furthermore, I had a career in politics, beginning with the Citizens' Committee for Harriman and Hogan in the Puerto Rican community; then the Committee for the Election of Robert Wagner, Mayor in his third term in 1960. Later I went on to direct the campaign for

John F. Kennedy in 1960, specifically for the New York Latino community and similarly for Robert Morgenthau when he ran for Governor. I also served on the Committee for the Election of Robert F. Kennedy, Senator for the State of New York in 1968. I was a delegate for the New York State Constitutional Convention and ran for Congress in the Twenty-Second Congressional District in 1964. For a person who started in the hope of studying medicine and becoming a doctor, I had truly taken "The Road Less Travelled" by Robert Frost:

> Two roads diverged in a yellow wood,
> And sorry I could not travel both
> And be one traveler, long I stood
> And looked down one as far as I could
> To where it bent in the undergrowth;
>
> Then took the other, as just as fair,
> And having perhaps the better claim,
> Because it was grassy and wanted wear;
> Though as for that the passing there
> Had worn them really about the same,
>
> And both that morning equally lay
> In leaves no step had trodden black.
> Oh, I kept the first for another day!
> Yet knowing how way leads on to way,
> I doubted if I should ever come back.

I shall be telling this with a sigh
Somewhere ages and ages hence:
Two roads diverged in a wood, and I—
I took the one less traveled by,
And that has made all the difference.

Although my mother had a third grade education, she steadfastly supported me, inspired me to make something of myself. She showcased me to the wealthy side of my family, the Carros, and my own success somehow vindicated her. The path I took to become a judge was arduous. My positions varied from being a busboy to welfare social investigator, to a social worker with the Youth Board, probation officer, police officer, street gang worker and a stint in politics. Along the way I attended law school at night and raised a family. I did not start out with the intention of becoming a lawyer; it was the furthest thing from my mind. I knew lawyers and my inclination was to view them as "pica pleitos," the Spanish equivalent of "ambulance chasers."

I have been consistent in my desire to serve the public and particularly my people. I was never really tempted by Wall Street offers nor did I take a job with the sole purpose of making money. I provided a stable, comfortable life for my family, which was far from lavish. Yet we understood that we were more fortunate than many others. To the extent that I attained power, I wielded it carefully and fairly. I never forgot the human beings who were affected by my decisions. Like my mother, I have tried to be the pioneer who leads others to better lives. I have always sought to use the positions I have attempted to make the way for other Puerto Ricans. Along the way, on occasion, I made history as in my experience with Sonia Sotomayor.

Judge Sotomayor began as a federal district court judge in New York and she was awarded the Hispanic Judge's Association John Carro Medal for Judicial Expertise. At the ceremony at Fordham University, she told the audience the story of her nomination to the federal bench. She was not the first choice of Senator Moynihan, but rather, it was me who was first nominated for the position. The chair of Moynihan's Judicial Committee, Judah Grivetz, had urged me to put my name in for the federal bench and I had finally agreed. All went well; I was approved by committees and given a high rating by the American Bar Association. I was endorsed by Senator D'Amato. My nomination was then sent to the Attorney General, Ed Meese, for submission to the White House, where trouble started. Firstly, I was a Democrat and was viewed as a liberal icon because of my agenda, particularly in regards to the advancement of minorities in the legal system. I was also for women's freedom of choice and took other positions that were an anathema to the Republican administration. There seemed to be no way that Bush would name me to be the first Puerto Rican federal court judge.

Because I was also endorsed by Senator D'Amato, a Republican, I had to go to Washington and be screened by Mr. Meese and his representative. During the interview, I was informed that I was too liberal and progressive and that my name would not be submitted despite being found highly qualified by the New York City Bar Association and the American Bar Association. They would neither reject nor forward my name to the White House, which was the prerogative of the Attorney General. My name would sit on the waiting list. It remained there for over three years, from 1989 to 1992. Senator Moynihan did not submit another name because he continued to support my appointment. After three years, I wrote to Senator Moynihan thanking him for his support and asked that he withdraw my name since it was unlikely that I would be appointed. I told him that I hoped that he would nominate another Puerto Rican for a seat on the federal bench. The Senator did as I asked and withdrew my name. In my place, he submitted the name of Sonia Sotomayor, who had been a former assistant district attorney in the county of New York. She was a Republican aid to the White House; she was highly qualified. She was a graduate of Princeton and Yale. When she was nominated I called to offer my congratulations and gave her advice about my experience in Washington. We have been good friends since then.

Justice Sotomayor went to sit on the federal district court of New York and after several years, applied for a vacancy on the Federal Circuit Court for the 2nd Circuit. Her nomination languished; blocked because of a decision that Justice Sotomayor made in the Wage Case, for which she was attacked by Rush Limbaugh. Limbaugh demanded that the Senator from Mississippi, who sat on the Judicial Committee, prevent her from appointment. No action was taken on the nomination until one week before it was due to expire. At that time, my firm, Carro, Velez and Battista, was contacted for help. I had retired from the judiciary and started a law firm that dealt with the advancement of Latinos. My partner, Das Velez had friends in the state legislature. Among them were Senator Efraim Gonzalez, who despite being a Democrat, had Republican contacts in Albany, and Senator D'Amato, who was running against a Democrat, Chuck Schumer. We told him the situation and advised him that supporting Judge Sotomayor's nomination would be politically advantageous in the Senate race which was quite close. At our urging, he took up the cause of Judge Sotomayor's nomination to the Circuit Court and, as a result, was cleared out of committee and received the appointment.

Sotomayor called Das and I to thank us personally. The rest was history. Judge Sotomayor was an outstanding jurist for the 2nd Circuit and was named to the U.S. Supreme Court by President Obama. I attended a reception given for her in New York, where I told her that I was happy to witness two things in my lifetime: one, the election of a black President, which I thought was years away, and two, the appointment of a Puerto Rican, among all the Latino groups in the country, to The Supreme Court of the United States. She continues to be a source of great pride for me.

Chapter Thirteen
Retirement from the Judiciary

I decided to retire from the judiciary in 1994, after 25 years; appointed as a judge of the Criminal Court in 1969 until 1975; acting Supreme Court Justice from June, 1975 to December, 1976; elected to the Supreme Court in 1979 (14-year term); named to the Appellate Division by Governor Mario Cuomo where I remained until my retirement in 1994. I decided to withdraw my name from a federal court judge nomination since it would not be forwarded to President Bush because I was too liberal and not what they wanted. My name was not submitted, but instead languished for three years until I contacted Senator Moynihan and asked him to withdraw my name while being investigated. I figured that I had accumulated forty years in city service and that my pension and social security benefits exceeded my salary if I stayed in the judiciary. I then decided to retire and return to private practice.

My retirement after 25 years of service in the judiciary was not the quiet affair I had envisioned. Thanks to two friends, Joe Wiscovich, a public relations professional and Bob Sacket, a private attorney, who orchestrated a bid sendoff in a retirement banquet at the Plaza Hotel, 58th Street and 6th Avenue, New York City. It was attended by over 400 invitees at $125 a ticket- wherein Haywood Burns from CUNY Law School as my keynote speaker, Frank Bonilla as my closest friend, Judith Kaye, Chief Justice of the N.Y. Court of Appeals, the Mayor of New York and many community and bar association people. It was a remarkable affair. I do not recall any other retiring judge being treated to such a spectacle.

Retirement Dinner at the Plaza Hotel - Keynote Address by the Late Haywood Burns

As an only child, I often say that I grew up lonely and wanted a large family. I have seven children and many grandchildren and they are a main part of my life. They have never let me down and I can honestly say that they "filled my cup" with happiness and pride.

Retirement Dinner with Honored Guests, Joe Wiscovich, J. Jose Cabranes, Bob Sacket and Robert Johnson

Terry and I with the Other Partners of Our Firm and their Wives

As I approach the twilight of my eventful and most enjoyable career, I am often asked what made me proudest of my life's accomplishments. I say "a happy and well-lived life." I am thankful to my heroes, beginning with my mother whose guidance, love, affection and ideals made me who I am today. My wife of all these years whom I love and cherish and who was always there for me and whom I credit for her love and raising of my wonderful children, Sherry, Christine, John, Greg, Lorna, Monique and Robert.

As for me, I will sum up my life with a quote from one of my favorite Latin poets, Pablo Neruda, who titled his biography, "Confieso Que he Vivido:" "I confess I have lived." Believe me, so have I.

Appendix

§ Keynote Address by the late Heywood Burns (attorney and dean, CUNY Law School) upon my retirement from the bench, Plaza Hotel, NYC, October 20, 1994

§ Remarks by J. Jose Cabranes (J. US Ct. Appeals 2d Cir.), at my retirement dinner, Plaza Hotel , NYC, October 20, 1994

§ Remarks by J. Sonia Sotomayor (J. US Sup. Ct.) recipient of the 'John Carro Award' given by the Association of Judges of Hispanic Heritage, Hispanic Heritage Awards Dinner, Columbia University, NYC, October 30, 2003

§ Noteworthy newspaper articles
"Temper Justice With Mercy" by John Carro, "New York Law Journal", Dec. 1, 1994

"Why Not the Best", "The Village Voice", vol. xxiii, no. 3, Jan. 16, 1978

§ Resume - John Carro

§ Professional Biography - John Carro

§ Selected poems by Luis Llorens Torres (Puerto Rican attorney, writer, poet)
"Valle de Collores"
"La Hija del Viejo Pancho"
"Palma Bruja"

§ Poem by Pablo Neruda (Chilean poet, diplomat, politician and Nobel Laureate in Literature)
"Veinte Poemas de Amor y
Una Canción Desesperada, Poema 20"

§ An excerpt from "The Little Prince" by Antoine de Saint-Exupéry

§ "Twelve Songs", #IX by WH Auden

§ An excerpt from "Romeo and Juliet" by William Shakespeare, Act 3, Scene 2

§ A quote by Ralph Waldo Emerson (American essayist and poet, 1803-1882)

§ Photos

Keynote Address by the Late Haywood Burns
(Attorney and Dean, CUNY Law School)
My Retirement from the Bench,
The Plaza Hotel, NYC
October 20, 1994

Keynote Address by Haywood Burns at
Retirement Dinner of Justice John Carro, Appellate Division, 1st Dept.
Plaza Hotel, New York City, October 20, 1994

JOHN CARRO and I were in the army together. In fact, we were in the army, the navy, the airforce and the marines together. Least you, good audience, think that he and I are some kind of closet militarists, or perhaps even worse, that John and I are somewhere even remotely close in age, let me hasten to explain that I first met John Carro in the early 1970s when he and I were both named to a Department of Defense Civilian/Military Task Force on Racial Justice in the Military. While I do not wholly subscribe to the popular belief that the term "military justice" is an oxymoron, military justice is, shall we say, different. It was my good fortune that I learned about it travelling the globe under Pentagon sponsorship, going into every branch of the service with John Carro, then a criminal court judge in the city of New York.

As National Director of the National Conference of Black Lawyers at this time, I had agreed to take on this assignment with great reservations. However, my colleagues and advisors prevailed upon me, wisely pointing out that probably never again would I get such an opportunity to penetrate so thoroughly the Department of Defense and the importance of having civilians among the generals and admirals who could write a minority report. As it turned out, we turned one of the generals, and we ended up penning the official Pentagon Report, with the dissent authored by the other military members of the task force.

Through it all I got to know John—to witness his intellectual acuity, his down to earth warmth, his unswerving, tough, dedication to principle. John, an ex-Navy swabble, seemed to take particular satisfaction in standing up to the Admiral, Judge Advocate General. In the end, I had made a friend for life. John is truly a remarkable human being--one of a kind, sui generis, as we say in the latinate language of the law. It is mete and proper and a wondrous occasion that has brought us, over 400 of John's friends, family, colleagues and associates, together to celebrate this great life, and to mark an important passage in it.

And a great life it is. Beginning in the hamlet of Orocovis in the central mountains of Puerto Rico, three score and seven years ago, John came to live on the border of Central Harlem and the Barrio at age 9, having never seen the sea. His first beach was Coney Island. He attended the New York City public schools, going to Benjamin Franklin High with someone named Daniel Patrick Moynihan. At the close of World War II, at the age of 18, he entered the US Navy. In 1949 two years after being honorably discharged from the Navy he entered the US Army Reserve, from which he was honorably discharged in 1954 as a First Lieutenant.

He served this city and its people variously as a social worker, a police officer (yes, John the cop); a probation officer whose charges included a young Lee Harvey Oswald (upon whom John unfortunately seemed to have left no long term impression); and a youth gang worker. Upon completion of law school he embarked upon a distinguished career in the private practice of law, with the pre-eminent attorney, now federal judge, Mary Johnson Lowe, as his partner. In 1960 he was tapped by Mayor Robert F. Wagner to serve as Assistant to the Mayor.

Named a Criminal Court Judge in 1969, John Carro has graced the benches of New York Courts for a quarter century, earning a deserved reputation as an outstanding, learned, and humane jurist. John Carro became an Acting Supreme Court Justice in 1975. He was elected to a full term as a Supreme Court Justice in 1977; and since 1979 he has been designated by Govs. Carey and Cuomo as an Associate Justice of the Appellate Division, First Department.

In 25 years on the bench he has left a lasting legacy in his jurisprudence. He has taken part in thousands of judicial decisions and written hundreds of decisions-whether in the majority or in dissent. It is an astounding body of work, at once too complicated and too nuanced to be easily summarized, but there are enduring themes that arise with constancy through his judicial work. There is the seriousness with which he takes the judging task. There is the respect and regard he has for his judicial colleagues and the process. There is a dedication to the lawyerly craft and high professional standards as is reflected in the drafting of his opinions.

There is his staunch constitutionalism, holding ground and fighting against the rising tides that would erode fundamental rights--particularly the right to privacy and the ever diminishing right to be free from unlawful search and seizures. In a different context, the first Mr. Justice Harlan, writing in the Civil Rights Cases in 1883, warned that unless our constitutional rights are to become what he called "splendid baubles, thrown out to delude those who deserved fair and generous treatment at the hands of the nation", there must be judges willing to stand up and protect and preserve them. Justice Carro has always been just such a justice. The courage of his convictions has been one of the most important hallmarks of his service in the judiciary.

3

Central to all that he has done as a judge, and I would add to all that he is as a person, is his compassion, humanity and sense of fairness. While fully grasping all that the law requires, John Carro has never lost touch with the realities of the world or the human condition. While a learned legal scholar, he has not forgotten the mean streets, or the role that race and economic status play in American life. He appreciates, far better than most, the irony in Anatole France's observation that, "The law in its majestic equality, forbids the rich as well as the poor to sleep under bridges, beg in the streets, and to steal bread."

We are all the fortunate beneficiaries of the corpus of Justice Carro's judicial work—whether in majority or in dissent, for his dissents, like his majority opinions, are models of lucidity, which like those of Holmes, Brandeis, Brennan, Marshall and other great dissenters of old, instruct us, challenge us, and serve as a beacon to illuminate the path to more enlightened times when today's dissents becomes part of tomorrow's consensus.

Justice Holmes once observed that life is action and passion and that one must share the action and passion of one's times or be deemed not to have lived. Judged by Holmes' standard John Carro has lived. He is certainly a person who has shared the action and passions of his times, entering life full throttle, immersing himself in the joys and agonies of our times, and doing all that he can to make a difference for positive social good. Tonight we celebrate his accomplishments, but we also celebrate the person.

All who know John know of his extraordinary zest for living. His appreciation of poetry and other forms of literature. His love of wine ... and song. His contemporaneity—up, not only on the latest cases, but on the latest movies, ready to discuss a Scalia opinion or what he thought of last night's screening of "Pulp Fiction" at the drop of a hat. He is a

4

citizen of the world, travelling the planet to China, Japan, Cuba, Argentina and elsewhere, usually in the cause of human rights. He is kind and generous without making a big show of these virtues. The story is still told of how, to the chagrin of authorities, when he left the criminal court bench he gave his entire McKinney's law books library to the inmates at Rikers Island. As they might say in various neighborhoods of this great city of ours: John is a "mensch;" a "caballero;" "John's down".

Among the qualities I admire about him most are his love of education and love of family. Education for himself and for others. John has an undergraduate degree from Fordham University and a law degree from Brooklyn Law School. Notwithstanding these excellent qualifications and his already demonstrated professional success, in the 1980's he furthered his formal education at the prestigious University of Virginia Law School, taking courses, writing a thesis, and earning a Master of Laws degree in 1984. He has taught at several campuses of the City University of New York and at Fordham University. He was one of the Founders of Aspira and the Puerto Rican Forum. He is on the Board of Trustees at Boricua College and on the Board of Visitors at the City University of New York School of Law. In the tradition of Eugenio Maria de Hostos, John places the highest premium on learning and never stops trying to acquire it for himself and to make it possible for others.

If you really want to see John light up, get him to talk about his family. He is so proud of his children and their accomplishments, and despite his desperately busy life, keeps up with their lives, and can regale you with stories about their doings at the slightest invitation. As he is proud of them, they are, I am sure, proud of him, and one could not have come this far without the love and support of the other. Can we all acknowledge John's family?

As a mirror to his soul, I recently asked John who are his personal heros? His answer was telling: Jefferson; Lincoln; Luis Munoz Marin; Don Pedro Albizu Campos; Justices Brennan & Marshall; Paul O'Dwyer and Ramsey Clark—all persons of tremendous personal courage, who took stands, sometimes unpopular, and stood by them in the interest of building a better world. That has been the story of John Carro's life and career to date. He has stood for the right, no matter what the personal cost. He has opened many doors for Latinos & Latinas, and has consistently been there through the years to come to the aid of, and to support and encourage other people of color. I know that John, even in his modesty, is proud of that. But what he is proudest of all is how he has served the whole people, without regard to hue; for at base, John is about humanity, the dignity and worth of all human beings and the importance of the triumph of the human spirit. It is in this sense that he likes to think of himself and deserves to be regarded as a "people's judge".

John has blazed the trail for those who come after. That we can salute with delight and revel in the successes of such distinguished jurists as my law school mate and friend Judge Cabranes and my dear friend Judge Ciparick, is in large measure a tribute to the ground broken by Judge Carro and others who have gone before them. And when we can, hopefully, in the not too distant future, raise our eyes to the highest court in the land and return the gaze of José or Carmen or some other brilliant Latino/a jurist sitting there, we will have the pioneering efforts of Justice John Carro to thank for having helped to make it all possible.

Moses did not get to the promised land. Dr. King did not get to the promised land. The New York City Court of Appeals and the federal bench were not so fortunate as to have

6

the august John Carro enhance their benches. It is their (and our) great loss.

As for John, it is a matter of no great moment. His entire life is a living monument to his greatness in the law; and it will continue with his life and the lives grown strong out of his life. I am sure that John knows this and is comfortable with it.

Further, it is an ever growing greatness, as John moves on to new arenas in the law; for we come this evening not to close a book, but only to close a chapter. The living monument of greatness will continue to grow and cause others to grow, because John is John. We celebrate this night a singular champion of the people who will continue, as he has always done to counterpose the complexity of law with the simplicity of justice; who has built bridges that others might cross; laid foundations upon which others might build; who bends with sure hands the arc of the dictates of the law toward the arc of the imperatives of justice, until they meet and form an arch under which we all can walk in dignity and peace.

The secret of John's success is his simple basic love of justice and commitment to be fair to others and true to himself. This simplicity is reflected in one of John's favorite poems by one of his favorite poets. The poem, "Valle de Collores". The poet, Luis Llorens Torres, who was himself a lawyer-poet of Puerto Rico.

The poem tells the story of a person who leaves his small country home and goes off to experience the life of the big city and experience it he does in all its multifaceted fast paced urbanity, but who in the end concludes it is not glory, or pleasure, or riches or power that really matter. That if it were in his hands he would erase his major triumphs in favor of a return on his little donkey or pony, "la jaca baya", to the good and simple life of fundamental values among the wildflowers of his country home.

The final two stanzas declare:

> Ay, la gloria es sueño vano.
> Y el placer, tan sólo viento.
> Y la riqueza, tormento.
> Y el poder, hosco gusano.
>
> Ay, si estuviera en mis manos
> borrar mis triunfos mayores,
> y a mi bohío de Collores
> volver en la jaca baya
> por el sendero entre mayas
> arropás de cundiamores.

Justice John Carro, as you ride off from the Court on your "jaca baya", though you leave the Court, your first name will always be "Justice".

Remarks by J. Jose Cabranes (J. US Ct. Appeals 2d Cir.)
Retirement Dinner, The Plaza Hotel, NYC
October 20, 1994

Remarks of Judge José A. Cabranes, of the
U.S. Court of Appeals for the Second Circuit,
at a Testimonial Dinner in Honor of
Justice John Carro
The Plaza, New York, NY
October 20, 1994

Distinguished members of the judiciary, members of the Bar, and friends:

It is a great pleasure for me to join in this extraordinary public tribute to Justice John Carro on the occasion of his retirement from the bench after 25 years of distinguished judicial service.

John Carro has been a pillar of the Hispanic community and an exemplar of public service for thirty-five years. It is hard to believe, I know, that he has been in la lucha for so long—especially for those who have observed the vigor and vitality with which he conducts his daily business.

But I well recall hearing of John and his work in the service of the community as long ago as 1960, from my late father, who served with John in the administration of the late Mayor Robert F. Wagner. That was in the era before the great fiscal and urban traumas of the late 1960's, when the government of the City of New York seemed—at least to this college student—a muscular and energetic and effective public force.

In that era it was well understood that the mayoralty of New York City was a politically more powerful and dynamic office than (for example) the Governorship of New York State—it had a larger budget, it performed many more public functions, and it employed

1

many more souls than any mere Governor. It was in that
era—which now, in retrospect, seems like a Golden Age of
Municipal Government—that John Carro as a young lawyer moved
into the front ranks of our public life. He never left
it—although, of course, by 1969 he had moved into another branch
of government.

It was in 1969 that Mayor John V. Lindsay appointed John
Carro to the bench of the Criminal Court of the City of New
York—from which he moved effortlessly in 1976 to the Supreme
Court of New York and, shortly thereafter, in 1979, by
designation of Governor Hugh L. Carey, to the Appellate Division,
First Department in Manhattan. There he has served with great
distinction ever since—for fully 15 years he has been New York's
leading Hispanic jurist.

The marvels of the computer age enable me to report to you
that, as of last week, John Carro's contributions to the
jurisprudence of New York State include no less than 16,832
entries in LEXIS, the computer law search service, and hundreds
of opinions he has written. This is a remarkable record of
productivity—and it will stand as only a part of his legacy to
the cause of justice.

I say that these decisions are only a part of his legacy to
the cause of justice because John Carro has left his imprint on
many other aspects of the law, including his notable extra-
curricular activities on behalf of human rights generally and the
Hispanic communities of the United States in particular.

2

I mention only one for the sake of brevity—his role as one of the founding members of the Puerto Rican Legal Defense and Education Fund, in which he lent his good name, his reputation, and his broad shoulders to a group of younger lawyers, who, I assure you, needed all the help and prestige they could possibly latch onto . . . .

There is one other aspect of John Carro's legacy that is not fully conveyed by a computer search of his decisions: his role as a pioneer of his community, breaking paths for others. John's career has been a string of "firsts"—and, when he was not the very first Hispanic in a particular position, he was surely one of the very first.

I do not exaggerate when I say that the many Hispanic jurists here this evening sit on the bench today because John Carro led the way—and, to his great personal credit, John Carro was always prepared to fight against what Justice Ruth Bader Ginsburg has called the "quota of one."

So, on this special occasion, John, I hope you will permit me, as one of the many beneficiaries of your path breaking efforts in our public life, to thank you and your family for your decades of public service, and to wish you many more years of professional and personal fulfillment.

¡Felicidades!

JACNYSPE.Jan1

Remarks by J. Sonia Sotomayor (J. US Sup. Ct.) Recipient of the 'John Carro Award' Given by the Association of Judges of Hispanic Heritage, Hispanic Heritage Awards Dinner, Columbia University, NYC October 30, 2003

Association of Judges of Hispanic Heritage
Hispanic Heritage Awards Dinner
October 30, 2003
Columbia Faculty House
The John Carro Award

REMARKS by HON SONIA SOTOMAYOR on 10/30 for upon receipt of John Carro Award

Rolando thank you for that lovely introduction. It is

incredibly wonderful to be in a room filled with family and

friends. I have received many awards in my life. Tonight is

particularly special to me, however, for two reasons.

First, this award is named in honor of a man, John

Carro, who was one of my idols when I started in the profession.

He was a judge of incredible principle and courage. He was a

champion of human rights and a supporter and promoter of our

Hispanic community's growth in the profession. Johnny's

commitment to our community and its well being led to my

appointment to the federal bench. Johnny withdrew his name

from consideration as a federal district court judge in order to

create an opening for the nomination of another Latino or

Latina.

I was fortunate enough to be Senator Moynihan's second

choice. To be second choice to a giant like John Carro

is truly an honor. That I can call a man with his integrity,

generosity and commitment a friend, is a tremendous privilege.

Second, I am being honored by Latino men and women, who

like John Carro, possess the highest integrity, are dedicated to

justice and committed to our community. That the Association

of Judges of Hispanic Heritage chooses to give me this award

touches me deeply not because it marks my professional success

but because it is being given to me by people who are friends

and who themselves haven given so much to our community and

the betterment of our world. This is a very deeply moving

honor.

In the last few years I have learned a very important

lesson in life -- professional success does not bring ultimate

happiness. What brings ultimate happiness is the quality of

sharing and giving that one experiences with family and friends

in the travels through one's life.

As most people in this audience know, I grew up in a

South Bronx housing project, the child of first generation

immigrant Puerto Ricans to NYC. As I grew, none of my

cousins in the states had yet graduated from college. I was,

however, a child with dreams. I dreamt first of graduating from

college and then from law school. I hoped to become a

prosecutor and, I even imagined that someday, if life was really

good to me, I would become a judge. The only kind of judge I

knew about then was a criminal court judge because my only

exposure to the law was from television and back then, Perry

Mason was the star TV attorney and he only practiced criminal

law.

Well, I have lived my dreams and more incredibly, I

have far surpassed them. With the help of family and friends, I

graduated from both college and law school, attending some of

the finest institutions in the land. I got to be a prosecutor in the

office of one of the finest DA's in the country, Bob Morgenthau.

I traveled the world in private practice as an international

commercial lawyer and I have become a judge.

I love my work. It stimulates and challenges me every

day. I wake up each morning excited about the prospect of

engaging in work that fulfills me and gives me a chance to have

a voice in the development of law. I love the law - I admire our

profession for all the good it has and continues to do in the

world. This award suggests that you perceive me as a

contributor to that good, and that is an honor indeed.

I have found great satisfaction in my life through my

work but it is not the measure of my success. I am successful

because I have been helped by so many people - my mom first

of all, by the dearest and most giving of friends - some who sit

with mom and many others throughout this room -- and by

people like Johnny Carro who opened doors for me, have taught

and guided me and shared their success with me.

Sharing life with loving and good people should have been the true dream of my childhood - I am glad to say that it is the dream and reality of my adulthood. If I can continue to say that I live a meaningful life because I do good work in which I give to others and I have family and friends who share my life with me and who give and let me give back to them, then I have truly succeeded far beyond my childhood dreams.

I take the honor of this award today and share it with all of you

in this room and the many family, other friends and even

strangers that have supported me through life. It is my hope that

as my life and work continue that I will live up to the high

standards of giving to others that all of you have set and that I

find a way to give more to others than I have received. Thanks

to all of you for the John Carro award and for continuing to give

me so much in my life. You, not me, earned any success I have

achieved

Noteworthy Newspaper Articles

"Temper Justice With Mercy" by John Carro, New York Law Journal" Dec. 1, 1994

NEW YORK LAW JOURNAL

PERSPECTIVE

Temper Justice With Mercy

BY JOHN CARRO

IN LIGHT OF MY RETIREMENT on Nov. 16, after 25 years as a jurist in the courts of this state, I have been asked to reflect on that experience.

I am first struck, indeed, persistently so, by my own personal odyssey. Coming to America from Puerto Rico at the age of nine, fatherless, speaking no English, growing up in the barrio in East Harlem ... to here. An American dream. And yet, as real as that dream has been for me, is it's failure for too many. Awareness of that failure has, I believe, informed my jurisprudence.

Of course, the courts cannot unilaterally right all wrongs and heal all social maladies. But the courts are often the cauldron into which social problems and transgressions are reposed for resolution — for some, final disposition. While some of our causative social problems have been addressed, at least in part over the last quarter century, far too many have festered. I have noted what has been a growing public intolerance and callousness to those whose actions violate the social contract. This intolerance and callousness in part has been reflected in the judiciary as well.

I would caution that we have grown too quick to criminalize that which merely, albeit understandably, offends us, and to enhance penalties without regard to deterrent effect, cost effectiveness and community protection. In observing our response to crime over the past quarter century, I can only hope that the future holds more places in the judiciary for women and minorities of all kinds.

Turning and turning in the widening gyre The falcon cannot hear the falconer; Things fall apart, the center cannot hold [.]

LIKE THE FALCON, our response to crime has grown more wild, distant from its causes and beyond earshot of reason. I see fewer and fewer remedies aimed at the roots of crime and more and more aimed at the simple fact of it. As we swell our prison space we constrict our social services to those, in a social sense, weakest and most in need. And, reminiscent of the Yeats' phrase, the center does not hold. Indeed, increasingly in drug cases I found myself questioning some perpetrators in light of the draconian sentences I had been forced by statutory mandate to join in sustaining.

In People v. Perez (134 A.D2d 455, 456), I questioned "whether the hemorrhage of taxpayer funds used to warehouse thousands of low-level drug users and sellers for long periods in our dangerously overcrowded prisons, at a cost of $35,000 per year per inmate in addition to the capital expenditure of $180,000 per prison cell, could not be more productively and humanely directed toward prevention, through education and treatment of drug addiction. The increasingly unavoidable conclusion that with the passage of time is becoming more widely recognized and articulated by respected representatives of our criminal justice system, is that the primary method currently utilized to deal with the drug epidemic, essentially an effort to eliminate the availability of drugs on our streets while increasing inordinately the length of prison terms for low-level drug offenders, has failed." Something is seriously wrong here, and the time to correct it is long overdue.

Also, of great concern to me have been the costs of legal fees in getting redress in the courts. When I came on the bench, with the exception in billing by large firms, small firms charged fees based on the case or monthly retainers. The trend is now towards hourly billing in the hundreds of dollars per hour to persons who seldom earn more than $15-$25 per hour. With these spiraling costs were rapidly creating two systems of justice one for the rich and the other for the poor. The so-called middle class can not afford counsel, and as in the health field, I can only hope that the medical insurance you can not afford to go to a hospital. Similarly people can not afford counsel to go to court.

AS THE FIRST and only Puerto Rican ever to rise to the Appellate Department of this State, I join in the call for diversity in the judiciary. I believe that government and the courts must come in composition to reflect the communities they serve, in this state particularly, that would lead to an inspiring diversity. I can only hope that the future holds more places in the judiciary for women and minorities of all kinds.

Indeed, I have been lured off the bench, in part, to the task of forming a largely minority law firm to provide enhanced opportunities in the profession for talented Hispanic and Latino, African-American, Asian-American and other minority attorneys. Just as others have opened doors for me throughout my youth and career, I wish to open doors for another generation. It is my objective to establish a major law firm providing a broad range of legal services, including corporate and commercial, while maintaining a commitment to diversity, public service and social responsibility.

As I leave the challenge of the judiciary for other challenges, there is some personal regret at my leaving the Appellate Division. For me, it was the greatest job in the world. Although I have loved and respected my colleagues, I have never hesitated to dissent when I deemed it necessary.

In all, I have been blessed and privileged to serve with luminaries and highly respected judges such as Samuel Silverman and the late Leonard Sandler and for that I am profoundly grateful.

In conclusion, the poet John Milton in "Paradise Lost," enjoined us to "temper Justice with Mercy." I should like to think that throughout my career on the bench, now come to an end, I never lost sight of that ideal.

John Carro, who retired as a justice of the Appellate Division, First Department on Nov. 16, is a partner with Carro, Batista & Velez, P.C. in Manhattan.

"Why Not the Best", "The Village Voice"
vol. xxiii, no. 3, Jan. 16, 1978

Copyright © 1978
The Village Voice Inc.   VOL. XXIII No. 3   THE WEEKLY NEWSPAPER OF NEW YORK   JANUARY 16, 1978   60¢

Why Not the Best?

It is not the purpose of this article to castigate the entire judiciary. Part of my motivation in naming individual judges is to avoid the generalized impression that all judges are unqualified.

In fact, there are more than a few of the city's approximately 350 judges who serve with distinction, who have reverence for the law, who are honest, courteous, unbiased, and hard working.

What follows is an admittedly incomplete honor roll of 20 trial judges who lend credit to their profession.

Peter McQuillan
Acting Manhattan supreme court

Bentley Kassal
Manhattan supreme court

James Leff
Manhattan supreme court

Ernst Rosenberger
Manhattan supreme court

Leonard Sandler
Manhattan supreme court

Arthur Blyn
Manhattan supreme court

Melvin Glass
criminal court

Martin Stecher
Manhattan supreme court

Irwin Brownstein
Brooklyn supreme court

Lawrence Bernstein
Acting Bronx Supreme Court

Israel Rubin
Bronx supreme court

Irving Lang
criminal court

Mary Johnson Lowe
Manhattan supreme court

Harold Rothwax
Acting Manhattan Supreme Court

Martin Evans
Manhattan supreme court

Sybil Hart Kooper
Brooklyn supreme court

John Carro
Manhattan supreme court

Thomas R. Jones
Brooklyn supreme court

Leon Polsky
court of claims

William Thompson
Brooklyn supreme court

—J.N.

Resume - John Carro

JOHN CARRO

24 N. DeBaun Ave. Apt# 103   475 Park Avenue South, 16th Fl.
Suffern, New York 10901   New York, New York 10016
Tel. (845) 354-7819   Tel. (212) 213-5005
                                    Fax (212) 213-5004

WORKING EXPERIENCE

1995 – present	Carro, Carro & Mitchell, LLP, Founder and Senior Partner. In November 1994, Justice Carro retired from the Bench after serving a total of 25 years. The last 15 years as the only Latino Justice in the Appellate Divisions of the Supreme Court of the State of New York. Justice Carro retired to form his own firm, which is now the largest Latino law firm in New York State.
1979 – 1994	Appellate Division, First Department, First Puerto Rican so named. Associate Justice, Designated by Governor Carey and subsequently by Governor Cuomo.
1977 – 1979	Justice, Supreme Court, First Judicial Department, elected to 14 year term. First Puerto Rican elected from the Bronx.
6/75 – 12/76	Acting Supreme Court Justice, Supreme Court First Judicial Department.
1969 – 1975	Judge, Criminal Court, City of New York
1967	Elected Delegate, 29th Senatorial District, New York State Constitutional Convention.
1960 – 1965	Assistant to the Mayor, Robert F. Wagner, City of New York. First Puerto Rican to serve in that capacity. Director of Mayor's Information Center – Mayor's Liaison for Social Services agencies. Sat for Mayor on Police and Fire Department Retirement Board.

Engaged in private practice of law from 1956-1969 when appointed to the Judiciary.

Former law partner of Mary Johnson Lowe who served in the Federal Court, Southern District, until her death several years ago.

TEACHING EXPERIENCE

1972 – 1983	Adjunct Professor, City College.
1983 – 1984	Adjunct Professor, Bronx Community College.
1980 – 1982	Adjunct Professor, Fordham University.
1977 – 1978	Adjunct Professor, Staten Island College.
1973 – 1975	Adjunct Associate Professor, Lehman College.

JOHN CARRO

EDUCATION

University of Virginia Law School – MA in Judicial Process, 1984.
National College of State Judiciary – Graduate Program, 1972.
National College of State Judiciary – Basic Program, 1970.
New York University School of Public Administration, Executive Program, 1963.
Brooklyn Law School – LLB, JD, 1956.
Fordham University – BS, 1949.

STATUS

Married with seven children - Sherry Lyn, Christine, Lorna, Monique, Gregory, John, and Robert - four of whom are attorneys. Gregory is a Court of Claims Justice; John is a partner in the firm Carro, Carro & Mitchell, LLP; Sherry Lyn is a former school teacher and now a government employee in Goshen, New York; Christine is secretary to Carmen Ciparick, Justice, Court of Appeals; Robert is assistant counsel. New York National Bank; Lorna is a pediatrician; and Monique is court attorney to Robert Sacket, Judge, Civil Court, Bronx.

ARMED SERVICES

United States Navy – 1945–1947.   Hospital Apprentice, First Class,
                                     Honorable Discharge.

U.S. Army Reserve – 1949-1954.   First Lieutenant, Honorable Discharge.

ORGANIZATIONS

P.R. Family Institute – Former Legal Counsel and Advisor
Hispanic Society – NYC – Police, Housing, Transit former Counsel and Legal Advisor
Boricua College – Vice Chair Board of Trustees.
Museo del Barrio – Member of the Board, Executive Committee.
New York State Bar Association – Member.
Supreme Court Justice's Association – Member.
Bronx Democratic County Committee's Independent Screening Panel for Civil and Supreme Courts – Former Counsel and Chairperson.
Association of Hispanic Judges – Founder and Former Chairman.
City University New York School of Law – Former Member, Visitors Board of Overseers.
Bronx Community College, Paralegal Studies Program – Former Chairman of Advisory Board.
Puerto Rican Bar Association – Founder and Former President.

Puerto Rican Forum – Founding Member, Former Member Board of Directors.

JOHN CARRO

Aspira – Founding Member, Former Chairman of Board.
Grand Council of Hispanic Societies in Civil Service – Founder, Former Counsel.
National Association for Puerto Rican Civil Rights – Former Counsel.
Puerto Rican Legal Defense Fund – Founding Member, Board of Directors.
HACER – McDonald's Advisory Board of Directors Former Member.
Latino Aids Commission – Former Chairman of the Board.
New York State's Advisory Counsel on Health Workers Testing – Former Member.
Governor Cuomo's Advisory Council on AIDS in Corrections – Former Member.
Community Service Society – Former Board Member.
The Legal Aid Society – Former Member, Board of Trustees.
The Appellate Defenders Office – Former Member, Board of Trustees.

ARTICLES

"Careers for Minorities"
The Puerto Rican Judge – Practicing Law Institute Book.

"The Structure of Legal Education and the Practice of Law in Socialist Cuba",
Master Thesis, April 1984. Virginia Law School – Judiciary Program. Thesis
published by Catholic University Law School Law Review, Ponce, Puerto Rico,
July-October 1985 edition.

LECTURES AND SPEECHES

University of Notre Dame, Cornell, Manhattan College, Temple Law School,
Rutgers Law School, Seton Hall Law School, Brooklyn Law School, New York
University School of Law, Northeastern Law School, Police Academy, New York
City, Hofstra Law School, Boricua College, John Jay College, Hostos Community
College, New York University, New York State's Legal Aid Society, District
Attorney's Association, New York State Trial Lawyer's Association, Association of
the Bar of the City of New York.

AWARDS AND HONORS

2003 CUNY Law School – Lifetime Service Achievement Award.

2002 Casita María Community Builder Award.

2002 Commonwealth of PR – Capitol, Lifetime Service Award.

1997 Honored as one of twelve Hispanics nationwide named "Pillars of Just Society", a program that recognizes professors, attorneys, and judges who have served the cause of justice in the Hispanic community, featured life story and photograph.

1997 Office of Court Administration, NYC Certificate of Appreciation – Housing Court Advisor Counsel – Search Community.

1996 New York State Criminal Defense Lawyers' Association - William J. Brennan, Jr. Award.

1996 Cardiovascular Association of Puerto Rico – Carnegie Hall Ceremony – School of Merit

1994 The Daily News - Hispanic Lifetime Achievement Award.

1994 Association of Bar – NYC – Certificate of Merit 25 years of Distinguished Judicia Service

1994 Puerto Rican Bar Association – Officers and Directors "Certificate of Appreciation"

1992 Hispanc Business Magazine – named as one of the "100 Influential Hispanics in the United States."

1992 New York University – Latino Achievement Award.

1992 New York State's Hispanic Heritage Committee - Community Service Award.

1991 Aspira Award for Project Leyes.

1987 Martin Luther King, Jr. Freedom Medal. Awarded by Governor Mario Cuomo

1987 Department of Corrections, State of New York – Award for Outside Support to Hispanics in Corrections.

1986 Hispanic Business Magazine – named as one of the "100 Influential Hispanics in the United States."

1985 Hispanic National Bar Association - Annual Award.

1984 Aetna Life and Casualty Company, American Opportunity Calendar, featured life story and photo.

1984 Hispanic Law Student Association, Brooklyn Law School.

1982 Boricua College, Roberto Clemente Award for service to the Hispanic Community in the Field of Law.

1980 John Jay College of Criminal Justice - Arthur Logan Award.

1980 Andrew Glover Youth Program – Annual Award.

1978 Urban Legal Studies Students Association at City College.

1977 Damas Unidas de America – Annual Award.

1976 Puerto Rican Bar Association – Annual Award.

1975 Puerto Rican Lawyers of Kings County.

1974 American Legion, Puerto Rican Day.

1964 Hispanic Society, Department of Corrections, City of New York, Annual Award.

1963 Hispanic Society, Housing Authority Police, City of New York, Annual Award.

1962 Hispanic Society, Police Department, City of New York, Annual Award.

RELATED EXPERIENCE

1992 – Japan Trip – Invited by Japanese Government, one of 30 Hispanics Selected from throughout US to visit Japan.

March 1981 – Visit to Puerto Rico as keynote speaker at 2nd Annual Conference of the National Association of Law Students. South, Central American and Caribbean students participated.

January 1978 – Visited the People's Republic of China as part of a Puerto Rican Community group invited to study the problems of health education and housing.

Professional Biography - John Carro

JUSTICE JOHN CARRO

Supreme Court, Appellate Division

First Department

Justice Carro, born in Puerto Rico in 1927, received a B.S. from Fordham University in 1949, a J.D. from Brooklyn Law School in 1956, admitted to practice before the U.S. Supreme Court in 1966, and received a M.A. from the University of Virginia in 1984. He served in the USN, 1945-1947, receiving an honorable discharge as 1st Lieutenant from the USAR in 1954. Justice Carro served as Assistant to former Mayor Robert F. Wagner from 1960 to 1965, the first Puerto Rican to serve in that office.

Justice Carro was appointed to the Criminal Court in 1969, became an Acting Supreme Court Justice in 1976, was elected a Supreme Court Justice in 1977, and was appointed by Governor Hugh L. Carey to the Appellate Division in 1979, becoming the first Puerto Rican to be designated an Appellate Division Justice and elected as a Supreme Court Justice from Bronx County. Justice Carro has been an adjunct professor with CUNY and Fordham University and is a founder and former Chairman of the Boards of the Puerto Rican Forum and Aspira, former board member of the Puerto Rican Legal Defense Fund, former President of the Puerto Rican Bar Association, and is now a member of the Supreme Court Justices Association, the Puerto Rican Bar Association, the National Hispanic Bar Association, the Board of the Museo del Barrio, the Board of Trustees of Boricua College and Lincoln Hall and Chairman of the Association of Hispanic Judges.

Justice Carro married the former Terry Parco in 1947 and seven children resulted from this union.

In 1987, Justice Carro was awarded the Martin Luther King Medal of Freedom by Governor Mario Cuomo. In January 1988, Senator Moynihan recommended him to President Reagan for appointment to the United States District Court for the Southern District of New York. If named, he will become the first Puerto Rican to serve in that capacity in New York State.

Poems by Luis Lloréns Torres

"Valle de Collores" by Luis Lloréns Torres

Cuando salí de Collores,
fue en una jaquita baya
por un sendero entre mayas
arropás de cundiamores.
Adiós malezas y flores
de la barranca del río,
y mis noches del bohío,
y aquella apacible calma,
y los viejos de mi alma,
y los hermanitos míos.

Qué pena la que sentía,
cuando hacia atrás yo miraba,
y una casa se alejaba,
y esa casa era la mía.
La última vez que volvía
los ojos, vi el blanco vuelo
de aquel maternal pañuelo
empapado con el zumo
del dolor. Más allá, humo
esfumándose en el cielo.

La campestre floración
era triste, opaca, mustia.
Y todo, como una angustia,
me apretaba el corazón.
La jaca, a su discreción,
iba a paso perezoso.
Zumbaba el viento, oloroso
a madreselvas y a pinos.
Y las ceibas del camino
parecían sauces llorosos.

No recuerdo cómo fue
(aquí la memoria pierdo).
Mas en mi oro de recuerdos,
recuerdo que al fin llegué:
la urbe, el teatro, el café,
la plaza, el parque, la acera...
Y en una novia hechicera,
hallé el ramaje encendido,
donde colgué el primer nido
de mi primera quimera.

Después, en pos de ideales.
Entonces, me hirió la envidia.
Y la calumnia y la insidia
y el odio de los mortales.
Y urdiendo sueños triunfales,
vi otra vez el blanco vuelo
de aquel maternal pañuelo
empapado con el zumo
del dolor. Lo demás, humo
esfumándose en el cielo.

Ay, la gloria es sueño vano.
Y el placer, tan solo viento.
Y la riqueza, tormento.
Y el poder, hosco gusano.
Ay, si estuviera en mis manos
borrar mis triunfos mayores,
y a mi bohío de Collores
volver en la jaca baya
por el sendero entre mayas
arropás de cundiamores.

"La Hija del Viejo Pancho" by Luis Lloréns Torres

Cuando canta en la enramada
mi buen gallo canagüey
y se cuela en el batey
el frío de la madrugada;
cuando la mansa bueyada
se despierta en el corral,
y los becerros berrear
se oyen debajo del rancho,
y la hija del viejo Pancho
va las vacas a ordeñar

entonces viene a mi hamaca
un olor como de selva
que no sé si esta en la yerba
o en las crines de las jacas
o en las ubres de las vacas
o en el estiércol del rancho
todo tiene un hondo y ancho
olor a felicidad;
y ese olor quien me lo da
es la hija del viejo Pancho.

"Palma Bruja" by Luis Lloréns Torres

PALMA BRUJA

Duermo en un segundo piso.
Frente a mi cuarto, una palma
se cimbra al viento de la noche
y casi se asoma por la ventana.
Yo la llamo Mercedes Salgado
(bien sé que no es nombre de palma).
La llamo Mercedes Salgado. Y le digo:
Mercedes Salgado, no seas mala;
abanícame, Mercedes Salgado,
con el lujoso varillaje de una rama;

y del racimo de tu seno,
dame a beber un coco de agua.
Ella se retequemenea, y a mis ojos,
baila que baila, baila que baila,
baila una rumba, una rumba de esas
que hacen temblar hasta la Habana,
mientras mi deseo besa y bebe
en el pezón del coco de agua.
Por instantes, la finjo
como si fuera, no una palma,
sino una real hembra morena,
indo-antillano-sevillana.
Le corre la morenería
desde los pies hasta la cara;
le corre la morenería
—Borinquen, Quisqueya, la Habana—,
le corre la morenería
desde la nuca hasta las nalgas.
Toda desnuda, toda la besan
el viento, el frío, la noche, el agua;
toda desnuda: toda vestida
de lunallena, de luna blanca.
La hinca el misterio de la noche
y casi se asoma por la ventana.
Tiemblan los cocos de su seno,
tiembla su cabello de ramas;
los cocos no parecen cocos,
la palma no parece palma.
Desde la fiebre de mi lecho,
se abren mis brazos y le hablan:
esta noche, Mercedes Salgado,
en que por ti corre la plata
de los luceros, y es la luna
copa de ron que se derrama;

esta noche en que yo te amo,
esta noche en que tú me amas;
esta noche, Mercedes Salgado,
Mercedes Salgado, no seas mala:
desembrújate de tu encantamiento,
y sé mujer, en vez de palma.

Poem by Pablo Neruda

"Veinte Poemas de Amor y Una Canción Desesperada, Poema 20" by Pablo Neruda

Puedo escribir los versos más tristes esta noche.
Escribir, por ejemplo: "La noche esta estrellada,
y tiritan, azules, los astros, a lo lejos".
El viento de la noche gira en el cielo y canta.
Puedo escribir los versos más tristes esta noche.
Yo la quise, y a veces ella también me quiso.
En las noches como ésta la tuve entre mis brazos.
La besé tantas veces bajo el cielo infinito.
Ella me quiso, a veces yo también la quería.
Cómo no haber amado sus grandes ojos fijos.
Puedo escribir los versos más tristes esta noche.
Pensar que no la tengo. Sentir que la he perdido.
Oír la noche inmensa, más inmensa sin ella.
Y el verso cae al alma como al pasto el rocío.
Qué importa que mi amor no pudiera guardarla.
La noche está estrellada y ella no está conmigo.
Eso es todo. A lo lejos alguien canta. A lo lejos.
Mi alma no se contenta con haberla perdido.
Como para acercarla mi mirada la busca.
Mi corazón la busca, y ella no está conmigo.
La misma noche que hace blanquear los mismos
árboles.
Nosotros, los de entonces, ya no somos los mismos.
Ya no la quiero, es cierto, pero cuánto la quise.
Mi voz buscaba el viento para tocar su oído.
De otro. Será de otro. Como antes de mis besos.
Su voz, su cuerpo claro. Sus ojos infinitos.
Ya no la quiero, es cierto, pero tal vez la quiero.
Es tan corto el amor, y es tan largo el olvido.
Porque en noches como esta la tuve entre mis brazos,
mi alma no se contenta con haberla perdido.
Aunque éste sea el último dolor que ella me causa,
y éstos sean los últimos versos que yo le escribo.

An excerpt from "The Little Prince"
by Antoine de Saint-Exupéry

"Here is my secret. It's quite simple: one sees clearly only with the heart. Anything essential is invisible to the eyes. People have forgotten this truth. But you mustn't forget it. You become responsible forever for what you've tamed. You're responsible for your rose..."

"Twelve Songs", #IX by WH Auden

Stop all the clocks, cut off the telephone,
Prevent the dog from barking with a juicy bone,
Silence the pianos and with muffled drum
Bring out the coffin, let the mourners come.

Let aeroplanes circle moaning overhead
Scribbling on the sky the message He Is Dead,
Put crêpe bows round the white necks of the public
doves,
Let the traffic policemen wear black cotton   gloves.

He was my North, my South, my East and   West,
My working week and Sunday rest,
My noon, my midnight, my talk, my song;
I thought that love would last forever: I was wrong.

The stars are not wanted now: put out every one;
Pack up the moon and dismantle the sun;
Pour away the ocean and sweep up the wood;
For nothing now can ever come to any good.

April 1936

An excerpt from "Romeo and Juliet"
by William Shakespeare, Act 3, Scene 2

"And when I shall die,
Take him and cut him out in little stars,
And he will make the face of heaven so fine
That all the world will be in love with night
And pay no worship to the garish sun."

A Quote by Ralph Waldo Emerson
(American Essayist and Poet, 1803-1882)

"What is success? To laugh often and much; to win the respect of intelligent people and the affection of children; to earn the appreciation of honest critics and endure the betrayal of false friends; to appreciate the beauty; to find the best in others; to leave the world a bit better, whether by a healthy child, a garden patch or a redeemed social condition; to know even one life has breathed easier because you have lived. This is to have succeeded!"

Photos

Appellate Division of the Supreme Court of the
State of New York, First Judicial Department
25th Street and Madison Avenue   New York City

Murals on East Wall of Courtroom L to R: "Justice of the Law" by Edward Simmons, "Wisdom" by Henry O. Walker, "Power of the Law" by Edwin H. Blashfield

Top Row: Smith, Ellerin, Kasal
1st Row: Mylonas, Ross, Kupferman, P.J. Murphy, Sullivan, Me,
Rosenberg

Campaign Director for JFK

On the Campaign Committee for Robert Kennedy

NYC Mayor John Lindsay

Left to Right: Monserrate, Badillo, Me, Mayor Lindsay, and Judge Nuñez

Left to Right: Jerry Lopez, Me, Boxer Rivera, Pete Hamill, and Ed Torres

Class of '84 Univ. of Virginia School of Law L.L.M. Degree Program for Judges

Greg's Swearing-In by Mayor Rudolph Giuliani

With my Sons John, Greg and Robert

Terry with our Daughters Monique, Christine and Sherry

Gregory's Swearing In Ceremony at Gracie Mansion with Mayor Rudolph Giuliani and Family

Members and Staff of My Law Firm

With Chief Justice Judith Kaye - NYS Court of Appeals

Our Firm (Circa 2000) - John Carro, Peter Quijano, Myself, Das Velez, and Bart Mitchell

At My Law Firm - Post Judicial Retirement

www.ingramcontent.com/pod-product-compliance
Lightning Source LLC
Chambersburg PA
CBHW030759150426
42813CB00068B/3256/J